Johnny Dakota and Travel Fish

Akaloo 1

Grades 3-4

by Darin Wiebe

Illustrated by Steve Skelton

ISBN-10: 0-8066-5732-4
ISBN-13: 978-0-8066-5732-5

Manufactured in the U.S.A.

Writer: Darin Wiebe
Editors: Dawn Rundman and Michelle L. N. Cook
Illustrator: Steve Skelton
Cover Design: Spunk Design Machine

Contents

Disciple

Church

Family

The Number-One Rule for Accidentally Traveling through Time

My name is Johnny Dakota. I'm eight years old and I travel through time. The number-one rule I have learned for traveling through time is—**never go alone.** When you travel through time you never know where you will end up. You just might need **help.** So **never go alone.** That's why I always take my best friend Ginny Stayput. My dog Stripe and my kid sister Molly come with us, too.

My best friend, my dog, my sister, and I all became time travelers by accident. It was all thanks to my sister Molly. We like to play in the vacant lot at the end of our street. We play baseball, hide-and-seek, kick the can, and all kinds of other games. But our favorite game to play is ARCHAEOLOGIST.

We dig holes all over the place to see what we can uncover. The second best thing we ever found was an old bowling ball. It was mostly black with some green swirls mixed in. There were chips in a few places and it had a long crack shaped like the letter "T." Ginny and I pretended it was a fossil of some old dinosaur poop.

The second best thing we ever found–Dinosaur poop fossil (aka old bowling ball)

Molly believed us for a while until she saw that the bowling ball had the name "Big Jerry" carved in it. Then she kind of blew up at us. "Do you expect me to believe that a dinosaur named Jerry wrote his name in his poop? Dinosaurs can't spell their names! Gosh."

But the double extra best thing we ever found came when Molly was crawling around on top of a big pile of old tires. I crabbed at her, "Get off that, Molly! You're gonna break your head bone or something, and Mom'll holler at me about it!"

She just looked at us and smiled. Then she jumped down inside the pile just like a bunny going down a hole. I called to Ginny, "C'mon! Let's go get her so I don't get in trouble." We started walking to the pile. Stripe trotted behind us.

While we were climbing up onto the pile of tires we heard Ginny yelling, "**Wow!** You guys come here!" She sounded just like she did on Christmas morning when she saw all those presents under the tree. Only now she sounded a little scared, too.

Stripe, Ginny, and I shimmied our way down through the dirty, worn-out tires. We couldn't believe our eyes. At the bottom of the pile of tires Molly had found something amazing.

Right in the center of the cave was a big, shiny, fish-shaped thing. It's not like it was a statue of a fish—it was just that it had the shape of a big fish. It sort of looked like a goldfish that wouldn't ever fit in a fish tank because it was so huge. It was as big as my dad's car. I got closer and looked at my reflection in the shiny side of the thing.

I jumped when I heard a loud creaking sound like a rusty door in a haunted house. Molly was opening a big door on its side. She whispered loudly, "Oh, man," and climbed in. Ginny and Stripe followed her into the side of the fish.

My knees were shaking and my feet weighed about 100 pounds each. I couldn't make them move! I didn't want my little sister to have more guts than me though, so I forced myself to climb in there.

Molly was already standing at the front of the fish, about where the brain would be in a real fish if a real fish was enormous and had a big squeaky door in its side and you could climb into it. Ginny stood next to her. "What is this thing?" she asked. She reached out to the dials and levers and buttons that glowed in front of us.

I tried to read some of the words by the dials, "Gen. Exo. Lev. What kind of language is that?"

Ginny got excited, "Those are abbreviations! This is English."

"Abbreviations for what?" I asked.

"I'm not sure," she answered. She tried reading some more of them. "Num. Deut." She bit her lip and thought.

Then the quiet was blown away when she hollered, "I've got it! Did you look at the Bible we got in church last Sunday?"

"Well, umm . . . I was gonna but . . ."

Molly interrupted me, "He hasn't looked at it one bit. His Bible's still next to the bread on the kitchen counter where he put it after we got home from church!"

I got ready to zing Molly but Ginny held up her hand and said, "I think these are abbreviations for books of the Bible. Johnny, run home quick and get yours."

Ginny's ideas are almost always better than mine so I almost always do what she says. I ran home faster than a cheetah with his tail on fire. There was my Bible, right on the counter where I left it. It was all fresh and crisp and unopened.

Ginny and Molly and Stripe were waiting for me. "Open it up to the table of contents," Ginny ordered.

I just stared at her.

"It's the page in the front that says what is in the book. Here, let me show you." I handed her the Bible and she opened right up to the front and showed me the list of books and their abbreviations.

"See," she said, "'Gen' is Genesis. That's the first book. 'Exo' is for Exodus, the next book."

I clicked the dial around to each abbreviation as she read them from the table of contents. "Yep," I told her, "they're all here in the same order as in the Bible. Thirty-nine clicks on the dial for thirty-nine books." I clicked it back to "Gen" for Genesis.

"Wait," said Molly, "there's another dial with abbreviations. What're those?"

"I'll bet those are the New Testament and the first dial is the Old Testament," Ginny answered. She read the names of the New Testament books and their abbreviations while I clicked the dial. Twenty-seven clicks for 27 books in the New Testament.

"But what are the buttons on the bottom for?" asked Molly.

Finally, a question I could answer! "I bet those are where you put numbers for chapters and verses for the books." I fiddled with the buttons and pushed one until a number popped up.

Molly yelled, "Let me!" She reached for the other buttons and pushed them. Then something else caught her attention.

She aimed her grubby finger at a purple button. Ginny sounded panicky and said, "Molly, maybe you shouldn't push tha . . ."

But it was too late. Molly pushed the button. The side of the fish squeaked shut all by itself.

Have you ever heard a robot burp? Neither have I. Actually, I'm not even sure a robot can burp. But if a robot could burp a loud, metallic, juicy belch, that's the sound we heard when Molly pushed the purple button.

God Has Dirty Fingernails

What are the parts of my Bible?

Pentateuch: Genesis—Deuteronomy

My nose hairs and my earlobes were all tingly, and I smelled the smell of sour apple gummy worms. The juicy robot belch was fading. "What just happened?" I asked.

A loud metallic clang filled the fish and we all screamed, "AAAAAAAH!" as its side opened up again. We stared out the door.

I tried talking but it was hard because my voice was all jiggly. "Th-that's not the tire pile."

"It's a forest," whispered Ginny.

Birds chirped, frogs croaked, bugs buzzed, and leaves rustled outside. We climbed out the door and stood in the forest where our empty lot used to be.

Stripe jumped out after us and ran ahead to what was the biggest tree I have ever seen. He stood on three legs and started to pee on it like it belonged to him.

"Did you hear that?" Ginny asked with a startled voice.

"What?" asked Molly. "The sound of Stripe peeing on a tree?"

"Shhh!" scolded Ginny. "Listen!"

In the middle of all the forest noises another sound joined in. It was the sound of a person whistling. Except it was like three whistlers blowing out of one set of lips. I know that sounds kind of weird but I can't think of another way to describe what we were hearing.

Do you know what dogs do when someone whistles? They run to them. And that's just what Stripe did. He took off running toward the sound. Molly cried, "Stripe! No! Come back!" And just like that she was running into the thick forest after him.

I got ready to holler and chase after Molly but a voice called out, "You mustn't leave Travel Fish without me."

I froze in my tracks. I looked around us to see who was talking. The only person I saw was Ginny. She was frozen in her spot, too. Her eyes were double extra wide like mine.

Now it was her voice's turn to sound all wiggly. "Who s-s-said that?"

The gentle voice called out again, "Please don't be

frightened. The child and dog will be safe. But you must not leave Travel Fish without me."

"Who are you?" I asked the voice. "And where are you?"

"I am Voice of Travel Fish. I have been programmed to inform you. You will find me inside Travel Fish. Please come back in."

Ginny went back in first, and I sort of leaned in and watched her. She asked, "Where are you?"

Voice of Travel Fish answered, "I am a small orange keychain shaped like Travel Fish. Look behind you." Ginny turned and saw the keychain hanging right there right in the open. The initials "VTF" were painted on its side in bright blue letters. "Take me down. Take the Bible as well. I will explain more to you as you go after the child and the dog."

We did what the voice asked us to do, trotting down a narrow path where Molly and Stripe had disappeared. As we went, the voice calmly told us that the machine we found was Travel Fish. VTF said that Travel Fish is a time and space machine that travels throughout the Bible. It can take people like my friends and me to different Bible stories so we can see and experience them in person.

We continued trotting down the trail. We could only see a little bit ahead of us on the trail. Beyond that we could see thick green leaves, colorful flowers, and tall trees. The whistling kept leading us.

VTF talked to us as we went along. She told us that there would be many surprises and mysteries for us if we decided to use Travel Fish to explore the Bible. She promised that she would be with us to help us get around and to explain some of the things we would read and experience.

Voice of Travel Fish asked, "Would you like to explore?"

"I just want to find my sister and dog," I said. "Mom'll kill me if anything happens to Molly. What will I tell my parents? 'This time machine called Travel Fish ate her?'"

"As I said, the child and dog are safe," VTF said.

Ginny asked a question that changed the subject. (Ginny always asks good questions.) "If Travel Fish travels through the Bible and we aren't in our vacant lot anymore, then where are we?"

"You are in the beginning. Travel Fish's dials were set to the book of Genesis, chapter 2, verse 4."

"I was right!" Ginny shouted. "Those dials were Bible passages! That means we're at . . ."

"There they are!" I interrupted her. Molly was on her hands and knees watching Stripe. He was digging like crazy, which is no surprise. That dog loves to dig! What was surprising was what, or who, was digging next to Stripe. It was our whistler.

A farmer wearing bib overalls and work boots was crouched down next to Stripe. Stripe was digging holes, and the farmer was putting in flowers!

Molly stopped walking. "Genesis," she whispered. "Are we in the Garden of Eden? Is this creation?"

VTF answered, "Correct."

"No," I argued. "Even I know that creation was when God said, 'Let there be stuff,' and stuff showed up just like he said."

"You are also correct," said Voice of Travel Fish.

"How can that be correct and this be correct?" Ginny asked. Thank goodness for Ginny and her questions. Not only does she ask the good ones, but she asks them at just the right time.

The answer VTF gave us may have been more confusing than the question. She calmly told us, "There are two creation stories. Both are true. In the first, God speaks and it is so. Our Creator is powerful and mighty. You are currently in the second creation story. Here, our Creator is present in creation through actions: planting and molding and forming all things."

"I don't get it. One says one thing. The other says something else," I complained.

"And yet, they say the same," VTF answered back. "Call the dog and child. Go back to Travel Fish. I will show you how both creation stories are true."

I whistled for Stripe. He stopped digging and ran to me.

"There you are," called Molly. She ran alongside Stripe.

Right here and now I need to tell you that my kid sister can talk faster than a rocket. Once she gets going, all you can do is listen and be quiet.

She took a big breath and started, "Do we know that farmer guy? I don't think I've ever seen him but it sure seems like I know him. Hey, did you hear him whistle? He sure can whistle! He said he whistles so good because whistling was his idea. He invented it. Hey! What's that you're holding, Ginny? Is that a keychain? That guy had dirty fingernails. He said they got dirty from working in the dirt."

When she stopped talking to take a breath we explained what we had learned from Voice of Travel Fish. And you know what? That kid didn't seem the least bit confused or surprised. All she said was, "Cool."

Back at Travel Fish, VTF told us to go to Psalm 24:1. She told us the Book of Psalms is in the Old Testament.

I clicked the first dial from Genesis to Psalms.

As I was clicking through, VTF told us that Psalms is a book of 150 prayers or songs. The people who wrote them wanted to talk to God about happy things, about sad things, and about how great God is. She told us we can use the psalms the same way today.

I got the dials set, and Molly started begging, "Oooh, ooh, can I push the button again? That was awesome!"

Before I could open my mouth to say yes or no, she pushed it and the whole place filled up with that juicy robot burp

My nose hairs and my earlobes were all tingly, and I smelled the smell of sour apple gummy worms. The juicy robot belch was fading. I'm not sure I'll get used to that.

When the door opened it was not a place that was outside Travel Fish. It was a color. It was every color at once. It was colors I have never even seen before. Voice of Travel Fish told us we could stay sitting and just listen.

Then a thousand happy voices said to us,

THE EARTH IS THE LORD'S AND ALL THAT IS IN IT, THE WORLD, AND THOSE WHO LIVE IN IT; FOR HE HAS FOUNDED IT ON THE SEAS, AND ESTABLISHED IT ON THE RIVERS.

"What does it tell you?" asked VTF.

Molly was the first one to understand. "It says that both creation stories say that God made the world. God is the boss of the world because God made it."

"Well done, child," VTF praised her. "Now, it is time for you to go home again. Push the red button above your heads. Travel Fish will take you back. It will remain where you found it. We are here for you. I hope you will use us again. There are so many adventures and mysteries waiting for you."

Molly begged again to be the one who pushed the button. I didn't bother answering her. She stood on her tippy toes and pushed the button.

The sound.
The tingling.
The smell.
We were home again.

How to Get Bear Drool out of Your Shirt

What are the parts of my Bible?
History Books: Joshua—Esther

None of us could wait to get back to the pile of tires in our empty lot. The next morning Ginny, Molly, and I raced back to the tires after breakfast. Even Stripe seemed excited to go with us.

There was Travel Fish, all shiny and red. Ginny put her hand on its side and the door whooshed open. We all climbed in and I took Voice of Travel Fish off her hook. Her eyes started to glow and she said, "Welcome back. I am pleased that you have returned." Her voice was calm and kind. "Where in the Bible shall we go today?" she asked.

"We hadn't thought of that," Ginny said. "Yesterday we went to Genesis 2 by accident."

"Yeah," Molly said. "We were just excited to get back to you today."

"I know where I want to go." I said. "I want to go to 1 Samuel."

Ginny looked surprised. "1 Samuel? Do you even

know what's in 1 Samuel? You're terrible at memorizing Bible verses."

I didn't get mad because Ginny wasn't being mean. I guess when you're good enough at being friends you can say stuff like that. She was right. My brains don't work so well when it comes to remembering stuff like that. I hardly ever remember which Bible stories go where. But this is one part of the Bible I remember.

"It's the story of David and Goliath," I said. "I remember them."

I didn't tell them that the reason I remember the story so well was because of Donnie Brook. Donnie Brook is the meanest kid in our school. He's in the third grade like me and Ginny but he's bigger than most of the fifth graders at our school. He always picks on me the most. When we learned about David and Goliath last year I imagined me being David and Donnie Brook being Goliath with a rock zinging from my slingshot straight to his head.

"Let's go see David."

Molly shouted, "I wanna set the dials! Where do we go?"

VTF answered her. "David meets Goliath in 1 Samuel, chapter 17."

Molly reached for the Old Testament dial and then stopped. "Uh oh. There is no 'First' Samuel. Only '1 Samuel.'"

"Don't panic, you goof. That's how '1 Samuel' is written—with the number 1. And you can begin with verse 1."

Molly frowned at me for calling her a goof. Then she concentrated on the dials and buttons. **Click, click, click,** to the book of 1 Samuel. **Click, click, click** to the chapter 17 button. One click of a button to verse 1.

She reached out to push the button that would zip us back to the story, but VTF stopped her. "I must warn you children. In order to truly meet David I shall take the liberty of carrying you to a point not long before 1 Samuel 17:1. You will find yourselves between the last verse of chapter 16 and the first verse of chapter 17.

"Wait!" Ginny shouted. "What happens there?"

But it was too late. Molly said, "Let's go!" and pushed the button.

We were surrounded by the juicy robot burp.

My nose hairs and my earlobes were all tingly, and I smelled the smell of sour apple gummy worms. The juicy robot belch was fading.

The door was already open and we looked out to a scrubby field. It smelled like spring and sheep were eating grass just outside

Travel Fish. They didn't seem to care that we had interrupted their breakfast. Stripe was already out of Travel Fish, sniffing around the sheep. They scolded him and trotted over to the next green patch. Striped barked and followed them.

"Look at Stripe!" Molly laughed. Stripe wasn't sniffing the sheep anymore. He was munching grass with them. We laughed and started walking over to him.

Suddenly the sheep ran away from us and Stripe started to bark and snarl and run toward us.

"Stripe! Wha . . ." I stopped because a growl from behind drowned out my voice and Stripe's barking. I spun around and saw a huge bear stretched over us. It looked hungry. It was drooling on my shoulder.

My knees wobbled and I tripped. The girls ran toward the sheep. I opened my mouth to yell but nothing came out. Stripe jumped over me and landed in front of the bear. Stripe's white and black hairs were standing up straight on his back. He growled and barked like I had never heard before. The bear howled and reached back to smack my dog! I closed my eyes tight.

A voice from behind me screamed, "YAAAH!" Then came a loud, "THWACK!" The bear yelped. When I finally had the guts to open my eyes, the bear was running away and Stripe was licking my face.

"Johnny! Did you see what that kid did? He threw a rock at that bear! Lookit! That hairy thing's still runnin'! Hey kid—where you learn to do that? What's that thing you used to throw the rock? Is that your slingshot? That was so cool! Can you show me how to do that? Huh?"

Molly kept on asking questions as the boy she was talking to bent down next to me. "Are you all right?" he asked.

"Yes. Are you . . . are you David?"

"Yes," he said. His voice was surprised. He had a few questions of his own. "How do you know this? Who are you? Have you been sent by the Lord to battle the Philistines? Why would the Lord send three children and a dog to go to battle? Ah! Who am I to question the mighty Lord? He shall deliver us as he chooses." He motioned to all of us. "Come with me. I am heading to the battle. I am delivering these supplies to my older brothers. They are soldiers. One day I will be a great soldier, too."

"You're going to be a soldier sooner than you think!" Molly told him.

"Oh, no," he told her. "I'm just a shepherd boy. I play my harp. I watch my sheep. That's all."

Ginny challenged David. "But didn't you just say that you shouldn't be surprised by who the Lord sends to deliver his people?"

"Yeah!" Molly added. "Just lookit how you chased that bear away from my brother!"

David argued, "The Philistine army is more powerful than one bear! They have a soldier named Goliath who is more than nine feet tall. He alone could kill that bear with his bare hands."

"The Philistine army *is* more powerful than a bear," said Ginny, "but our mighty Lord is more powerful than a thousand armies."

David stopped. "These are wise words. Only a messenger of the Lord can say such things. Now I am certain that the living God has sent you to defeat Goliath."

I said, "Well David, we honestly can tell you what God will do." (This is the only Bible story I know by heart, so I told him what was going to happen next.) "When we arrive at the battle, your oldest brother will get real mad at you. He'll say you're just there to see the battle and he'll accuse you of leaving your sheep all alone. Goliath will come out and say nasty things about Israel and God. But no one will have the guts to do anything about it."

Molly added, "But you'll have the guts, David!"

"It was the living God who saved you from that bear, David," Ginny said. "And God has saved you from other bears—and lions, too."

I said, "When these things happen you'll know we are right, David. And God will use you to save your people from Goliath just like you've saved your sheep."

We all walked for a long, long time without saying a word. It seemed like hours until we got to the camp where Israel's army was watching the Philistine army.

David ran ahead to some men while we sat down to rest. We couldn't hear what they were saying but it was obvious that one of them was angry with David. He kept pointing back to the direction we came from.

"That must be his oldest brother yelling at him," said Ginny.

"That's what big brothers do best," Molly said. "Hey Johnny, you could be in the Bible!" And she socked me in the arm.

David was crabbing back at his brother when Goliath stepped up to the front of his army. He was huge! He was bigger than anyone you have ever seen in your life. He started shouting nasty things about God and God's people.

David turned and stared at us. He knew. He knew we were right. He knew that God would use a shepherd boy to defeat Goliath.

Now David and the others were walking toward us. They were arguing again. One of the men was telling David that he could never defeat Goliath because he was just a kid.

David reminded them that he had fought lions and bears while protecting the sheep. "Each time, God delivered me from the paws of those beasts!"

Before you could pick up five smooth stones, they were handing David a sword and putting armor on him. David tried walking, but the sword was dragging on the ground. The armor was hanging crooked off his shoulder. It looked like a bad Halloween costume.

Molly shot up like a rocket and ran toward David. Several soldiers tried to stop her, but that kid's squirrelly. If she wants to get away from you, she will. When she reached David she stood on her tippy toes and whispered in his ear. He smiled. As she ran back to us David began to take off the oversize armor.

Ginny asked, "What did you say to him?"

"I told him to use his slingshot."

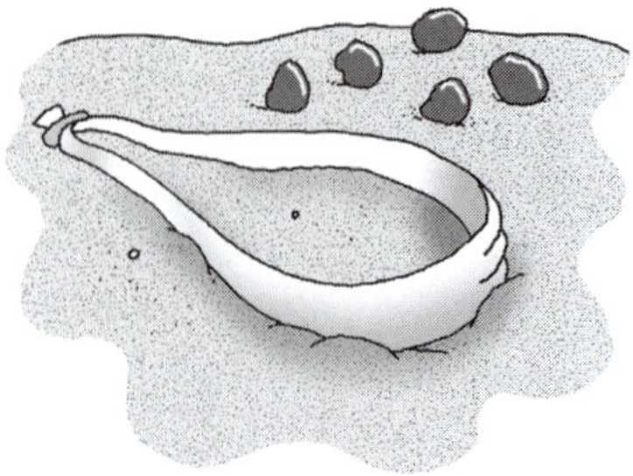

We watched David pick up some stones. One. Two. Three. Four. Five. He took his slingshot out and walked toward the giant.

Goliath pointed and laughed at David. I swear, he was laughing so hard that if he had been drinking milk it would have shot out his nose!

David was calm. He put the first stone in the sling. He yelled, **"YAAAH!"** as he swung his arm backward in one smooth circle. Then came a loud, **"THWACK!"**

Goliath looked surprised as he slapped his hand on his forehead. He crumpled down like a tower.

The Philistine army ran away. God's army cheered. Voice of Travel Fish spoke in the middle of all the noise and confusion. "Children, we must leave now. Quickly."

I knew what was going to happen next. Goliath was going to lose his head. I really didn't want to see that. Travel Fish had appeared behind us. Its door was open and waiting for us.

Even when the door was shut behind us we could hear the army cheering and celebrating.

VTF asked, "What did you learn today, children?"

"To start carrying a slingshot!" Molly exclaimed.

Ginny said, "It wasn't about beating Goliath with a slingshot so much as it was about trusting God to take care of him. When David trusted God, he could do impossible, scary things."

“Well done, children,” said VTF. “Molly, would you please push the red button?”

Molly didn’t have to be asked twice.

We were surrounded by the juicy robot burp.

My nose hairs and my earlobes were all tingly, and I smelled the smell of sour apple gummy worms. The juicy robot belch was fading. We were home again.

My First Ever Psalm of Lament

What are the parts of my Bible?
Poetry Books: Job—Song of Solomon

There is a voice I dread hearing. It is the voice of Donnie Brook. He's the meanest kid in the third grade. He's the meanest kid in the whole school. There are fifth graders who are scared of him. And out of a whole entire grade school full of kids to pick on, I am his favorite target.

One afternoon Molly, Ginny, Stripe, and I were leaving the empty lot where we play and I heard that voice. "Hey ladies! Where do you think you're going?"

Donnie Brook.

I did what I always do when Donnie starts to pick on me. I ignored him and I kept walking home. Only I walked a little faster than before.

What Donnie Brook does best is insults. And his best insult is to take your name and change it into something mean. "Hey! I'm talking to you, **Duh-ko-duh!** You better stop."

By now he was standing right in front of us. The only thing we could do was stop and listen to his insults. "What were you doin' in the pile of tires—playin' with yer dollies? HA! Johnny **Duh-ko-duh** was playin' dollies with the other girls!"

Molly stepped in between Donnie Brook and me. "Why don't you leave us alone Donnie Ding-a-ling! And for your information, we weren't playing dollies! We were with Travel Fish and we traveled in the Bi . . ." I grabbed her from behind and covered her big mouth with my hand.

I don't know what was worse: that my kid sister just called the school bully a ding-a-ling or that she almost told him about Travel Fish. Either way, I wanted her to stop before it was too late.

But it was too late. Donnie stared at us. He looked confused and he looked angry. That's a bad combination in a dim kid like him. I think I saw steam coming out of his ears. "What did you say?"

My mind was racing a million miles an hour. Travel Fish was going to be hard enough to explain. How would we explain it to a gorilla like Donnie Brook?

He growled at Molly, "What did you call me?" Then he looked over her head at me, "Hey **Duh-ko-duh,** does your baby sister protect you all the time? Look at you, hiding behind the baby!" Then he reached over her and pushed me down onto the ground and stomped away.

Stripe sat next to me and licked my face. I looked at him and said, "Just once in a while I wish you'd be a mean dog and tear a hole in the back of Donnie Brook's pants." Stripe looked at Donnie walking away from us. He looked back at me and whimpered.

I stared down at the dirt where I was sitting. I hate it when Donnie does mean stuff like this. The top of my head felt real hot. My eyes were all stingy. I was afraid that if I looked at Molly and Ginny I would start bawling.

Molly asked, "Are you cryin' Johnny?"

"NO!" I said it so rough it made my throat hurt. I got up quickly and started walking toward home.

Ginny, Molly, and Stripe all caught up with me. For a while we just walked without talking. Then Molly couldn't hold it in anymore. "Hey! We could trick Donnie Brook into Travel Fish and take him to the Bible story about David and Goliath and once David takes care of ol' Goliath he could knock Donnie Brook in the head with his slingshot! **POW!** Right in the melon. Wouldn't that be great?"

"Woof!" Stripe agreed.

"Donnie Brook is the worst," I said. "I wish I could knock him over. I'd push him down in front of *his* friends. Only he doesn't have any friends on account of he smells like burnt pickles and he never changes his underwear."

I was on a roll. I was getting louder with every sentence. "I wish he'd get hit by a meteorite! I wish a satellite would crash from outer space and land on his head!"

"Maybe you should settle down a bit," Ginny warned.

"Yea," Molly added. "You're so mad that there's spit coming out of your mouth."

"What, can't I be mad?" I asked.

Ginny said, "Sure you can be mad. I just don't think you should be saying and wishing such nasty things. Not even about Donnie Brook."

"Yeah," Molly whispered. "You're kinda' scarin' me."

I breathed out a big sigh. "I'm sorry I scared you. But if I can't talk to you like this, then who?"

"Well," Ginny said, "tell God what you're thinking."

"Are you crazy?" I whispered. "That's no way to talk to God."

Ginny asked, "What do you mean? How do you think we're supposed to talk to God?"

"You know . . ." I whined. "You're supposed ask God for stuff and say things like 'thanks for the flowers' and prayers like that. But I don't think that you're supposed to gripe at God."

"There have to be more kinds of prayers than that," Ginny said.

"Let's go ask Travel Fish," said Molly.

So we did. We explained the situation to VTF. She asked us to set the dial to Psalm 13.

Molly pushed the purple button.

We were surrounded by the juicy robot burp.

My nose hairs and my earlobes were all tingly, and I

smelled the smell of sour apple gummy worms. The juicy robot belch was fading.

We had been to the book of Psalms before. In the book of Psalms, when the door opens it is not a place that's outside the Travel Fish. It is color. It is every color at once, even colors I have never even seen before.

We sat back and listened as a single voice spoke. It sounded like it was coming from very far away and talking through a tin can.

> How long, O Lord? Will you forget me forever?
> How long will you hide your face from me?
> How long must I bear pain in my soul,
> and have sorrow in my heart all day long?
> How long shall my enemy be exalted over me?

Then the voice started to get closer and sounded clearer.

> Consider and answer me, O Lord my God!
> Give light to my eyes,
> or I will sleep the sleep of death,
> and my enemy will say, "I have prevailed";
> my foes will rejoice because I am shaken.

Finally the voice was right there with us, and it sounded clear as day.

But I trusted in your steadfast love;
my heart shall rejoice in your salvation.
I will sing to the Lord, because he has dealt bountifully with me.

After we got back to the empty lot VTF showed us a pattern in the Psalm. "That was a psalm of lament. There are many of them in the Bible. *Lament* means you are telling God that you are sad or angry or scared or all three.

"When the voice was far away, it listed complaints to God. The voice even questioned God about taking so long to help. Then the prayer asked God for help. Finally, the prayer remembered that God has helped in the past and will help again.

"Your God is big. God loves you and wants to hear from you. You may say whatever you think to God."

So that night at bedtime I prayed my first ever psalm of lament:

Every time, God;
Every time I see Donnie Brook, he clobbers me.
Why don't you do anything?

How many times will you let him knock me over?
Won't you do something?
How many times will he get to embarrass me?
Won't you do something?

I know that you've taken good care of me
in the past.
I know you are bigger than Donnie Brook.
I have a family and a warm bed.
I know you will take care of me
in the future.
So now I'll lay me down to sleep
And you will protect me tonight.

I crawled into bed. I listened to Stripe breathing himself to sleep on the floor under my bed. I fell asleep.

The OT Prophets Lineup

What are the parts of my Bible?

Prophetic Books: Isaiah—Malachi

After Travel Fish brought us home, we stayed inside it for a while. We talked about everything we had just seen with David. But sitting and talking is never good enough for my kid sister. She had to go and touch another button.

Lucky for all of us, the button she pushed didn't send us into outer space or some crazy place like that. The blue button she pushed opened up a small compartment in front of us. It was sort of like the glove compartment in my mom's minivan. The door popped open and out flew a bunch of baseball cards. At least that's what they looked like.

We picked them up and looked at each of them. They were cards for a team called The OT Prophets.

"That's not a team I've ever heard of," I said.

Voice of Travel Fish spoke up. "The cards are for prophets from the Old Testament. The Old Testament is the first part of your Bible, the part written before Jesus was born."

"What's a prophet?" Molly asked.

I wasn't surprised that Ginny knew the answer. "Prophets were people that God picked. Then God had them bring messages to the rest of the people."

"That is correct," VTF told her. "Almost every prophet was scared to do as God asked. They gave God many excuses about why they were the wrong people to speak for the Lord."

"What kind of excuses?" I asked.

"Some thought they were too young. Others said they could not speak well enough or that they were just sheep herders and could never do anything such as speak for God. God asked them to bring harsh news to the people. God was angry with his people because some had stopped worshiping God. Others were cruel to the poor."

"I suppose that being a prophet *would* be a hard job," I said.

"Certainly, but do you recall how David defeated Goliath? Was it his skill with the slingshot?" VTF asked me.

"No," I said. "It was that he trusted God to protect him and help him."

"That is the same promise God gave to the prophets. God would go with them and give them the words to speak," said VTF.

Anyway, here are a bunch of the cards we found in Travel Fish's glove compartment.

Isaiah Rookie Card

Nickname: Ol' Fire & Brimstone

Claim to Fame: Early in his career Isaiah was a hard hitter, railing against the people for trusting everything and everyone *but* God.

Listen Here: (Isaiah 5:25) Therefore the anger of the Lord was kindled against his people, and he stretched out his hand against them and struck them.

Isaiah Veteran Card

Nickname: Suffering Servant

Claim to Fame: As a seasoned prophet, Isaiah's words began to point to Christ who would bring forgiveness and light to a scary world.

Listen Here: (Isaiah 60:1) Arise, shine; for your light has come, and the glory of the Lord has risen upon you.

Jeremiah

Nickname: The Kid

Claim to Fame: This slugger was called up to the big league prophets at about age 13. He told Israel that if they didn't turn away from idols and worship only God, Babylon's army would take over. His prophecy came true.

Listen Here: (Jeremiah 29:11-12) For surely I know the plans I have for you, says the Lord, plans for your welfare and not for harm, to give you a future with hope.

Ezekiel

Nickname: Boneyard Dog

Claim to Fame: He told God's message of new life to a bunch of dead bones. Then came the sound of rattling bones putting on skin like you put on jammies. God doesn't wait for us to ask for help but comes to help us when we can't even ask for it.

Listen Here: (Ezekiel 37:4-5) O dry bones, hear the word of the Lord . . . I will cause breath to enter you, and you shall live.

Daniel

Nickname: The Lion Tamer

Claim to Fame: You can't keep this kid down! Daniel was commanded to pray only to the king but he prayed to God instead. His punishment: spend a night in a lion's pit. God sent an angel to hold the lions' mouths shut. Daniel slept well that night.

Listen Here: (Daniel 6:23) So Daniel was taken up out of the den, and no kind of harm was found on him, because he had trusted in his God.

Amos

Nickname: Wooly Bully

Claim to Fame: Amos was a sheep herder who got called up to the big league prophets to tell his people to care for the poor. In his time, Israel was very religious. But even though they were rich, they were mean to poor people.

Listen Here: (Amos 2:6) God was mad at Israel because they sold people "for silver, and the needy for a pair of sandals . . ."

Jonah

Nickname: Fish Guts

Claim to Fame: Most people know that Jonah was swallowed by a large fish, but did you know that the fish also puked Jonah onto dry land? See for yourself at Jonah 2:10.

Listen Here: (Jonah 2:1, 9) Then Jonah prayed to the Lord his God from the belly of the fish . . . "Deliverance belongs to the Lord!"

Little Jesus Lost

What are the parts of my Bible?

Gospels: Matthew—John

My sister Molly, my best friend Ginny, and I had been though many adventures in Travel Fish. We were beginning to feel right at home inside of it. Some days we just sat inside Travel Fish and talked—without going anywhere. That's what we were doing one cloudy day. Stripe was sleeping on one of the seats just like he sleeps on his favorite chair at our house. Ginny was smiling and shaking her head as Molly and I argued about which one of us was meaner.

Voice of Travel Fish interrupted us. "Children, it is time."

"Time for what?" Ginny asked as she reached for the little fish key chain that led us and helped us in our Bible travels.

"Travel Fish has brought you many places in the Bible. But so far you have only ventured into the Old Testament. You have seen how the Lord has made the world and everything in it, including you. You have seen the many ways God has sought to bring his people back to him. The prophets, the poets, the kings. Now you will enter the New Testament. Now you will see and experience Jesus, the Son of God."

"Wow!" Molly exclaimed. "Will we see him as a baby or as a grown up?"

VTF said, "Neither." VTF has a way of answering without ever really giving us information.

"How can he be neither a baby or a grown up?" I asked.

"That will be your adventure this time, children. Luke, chapter 2, verse 41 will be able to answer your question."

Molly didn't miss a beat. She jumped right to the dials and buttons and clicked them to Luke 2:41. For the first time we were using the New Testament dial.

My nose hairs and my earlobes were all tingly, and I smelled the smell of sour apple gummy worms. The juicy robot belch was fading.

Travel Fish's door opened up to show us a back alley in a busy city. Ginny asked VTF, "Where are we?"

"You are in Jerusalem. The city is more busy than usual because it is the festival of the Passover."

"The what of the who-over?" asked Molly.

VTF went on, "The festival of the Passover is a religious holiday. Jewish people all over the world still celebrate that your Heavenly Father saved them from slavery in Egypt. During Jesus' time, many Jewish people celebrated Passover by traveling to Jerusalem and worshiping at the temple. I believe now would be a good time for you to look for the temple and see what is happening there."

I had a question that I thought would stump VTF. "Wait a second. It was in the Old Testament that God saved the Jewish people from slavery. If Jesus is in the New Testament, what does he have to do with the Passover?"

VTF was quick with the answer. "Jesus Christ was born a Jew. It was his custom to celebrate this important Jewish holiday."

"Oh," I said. "Okay."

We walked into the street and began to follow the crowd. We soon walked up to a large walled yard, sort of like a fort. People milled in and out of it. Some looked bored, some were crying, some were laughing.

"This is the temple, children. Your dog will not be able to go in," VTF warned. "If you clip me to his collar, we shall both be safe out here."

I asked Stripe if he thought this would be okay. He wagged his tail as I clipped VTF on his collar. We didn't know what to expect as we walked into the temple. But we had learned to trust what Voice of Travel Fish told us. So we walked in the big gate.

Inside, it was open, like we were in someone's big front yard. In the rear of the big yard was a long tall building. We didn't see as many people inside as we saw outside. That made it easy to spot a crowd on the steps in front of the building.

Molly was the first to see. "Hey, look at all those old guys yelling at that kid!"

Ginny pointed out, "They're not yelling at him. They're listening to him." The men looked like pastors or professors or somebody like that.

We moved closer so we could listen. The boy was talking about Isaiah, one of the prophets from the Old Testament. He told them about creation and about the Ark. The men asked him questions about God, and he was answering them. He had questions for them, too. They seemed to be pretty impressed with him.

"Wait a second," Ginny gasped, "that's not just any kid. That's Jesus. See? He's not a baby. He's not a grown

up. He's a kid. I bet he's only a couple of years older than us, Johnny."

"Cool!" said Molly. "Jesus was a kid like us."

"Yeah, I always just thought about him as a baby or a grown up," I told her.

Ginny said, "Jesus is God. So if Jesus was a kid like us . . . then God was a kid—for a while at least. That is so cool! God knows what it's like to be a kid."

Molly had a thousand questions. "Do you think he had a favorite toy? Did he have his own bedroom? I wonder if he got straight A's in school."

I asked, "I wonder if he had a nosy little sister?"

Molly was getting ready to holler at me but she was interrupted by a ruckus at the front gate of the temple.

"Oh! There he is! Jesus! Jesus! Where have you been?" A lady was shouting and crying and running toward him.

"That must be Mary," observed Ginny.

"We've been looking for you for three days!"

I couldn't quite tell if Jesus was in trouble or if his mom was just really happy to see him.

But Jesus didn't look worried. He looked kind of serious when he answered her. "Why were you looking for me? Didn't you know that I must be in my Father's house?"

"He's not talking about Joseph," whispered Ginny. "This is the temple, God's house. God is his Father. That's why he knows so much."

"Yeah," I said, "he knows about creation because he was there."

The men stood up and let Mary hug Jesus. She shuffled her son into the crowd of people who had come in with her. Suddenly Jesus blended in with other kids and grown-ups. Those must have been his cousins and brothers and sisters, aunts and uncles. His family.

"Let's go out with them," said Ginny. We shuffled out behind the crowd.

Jesus was talking with his mom. "They were surprised that I know so much. They thought I was tricking them."

"I think you'll be here again," Mary said. "Some of them may be here then, too."

We all continued to walk out of the temple yard. Jesus and his family continued to walk on when we stopped to get Stripe and Voice of Travel Fish. VTF asked, "What did you see, children?"

We told her about the boy Jesus and how he was teaching the teachers. She was impressed that we were able to figure out what we were seeing without her telling us.

We climbed back into Travel Fish; Molly pushed the button to go home.

My nose hairs and my earlobes were all tingly, and I smelled the smell of sour apple gummy worms. The juicy robot belch was fading. We were home again.

Walking under Water

What are the parts of my Bible?

Adventure Stories: Acts

One Sunday after church I was hanging out in the cockpit of Travel Fish along with my kid sister Molly and my best friend Ginny. My dalmatian Stripe was curled up in a corner taking a snooze. We weren't planning on a trip or anything. It was just a good place to be.

But Molly can only take so much hanging around. "I'm bored," she complained. "Let's do something fun. Let's go somewhere. Let's meet someone else in the Bible. Let's go on an adventure!"

Now I'm the first person to admit that we had been to some cool places in the Bible. We saw God planting stuff at creation. We saw David sling his rock at Goliath. But adventure didn't seem like the right word. "There's good stuff in the Bible, Molly. But I don't know about adventure. There weren't any roller coasters or astronauts in the Bible."

That must have woken up Voice of Travel Fish. She was hanging from her hook when she spoke to us. "You may be surprised by the adventures in the Scriptures. I have been instructed to keep you away from certain places in the Bible that are too dangerous for you."

"Where's that?" Molly yelled. "That's where I want to go!"

"Oh, there are prisons and battles and places of great danger and pain. They are no place for you, child."

"C'mon, VTF!" my little sister begged. "We want *adventure*!"

Ginny added, "It could be fun. Johnny could learn a thing or two about the Bible, VTF. Isn't there some place a little bit wild where you could take us?"

VTF seemed to be thinking it through. "Prepare to travel. Set the New Testament dial to the book of Acts, chapter 27, verse 42."

Molly was eager for adventure. She jumped to the dashboard and clicked the dials and buttons to Acts 27:42. As Molly reached for the button, Voice of Travel Fish spoke. "Be careful children. Hold on." VTF sounded worried.

The juicy robot burp surrounded us.

Water instantly crashed into the cockpit! Over the rush of the water we heard a scared, angry voice shout,

"KILL THEM NOW!"

The water flushed us out of Travel Fish like it was a toilet. We ended up on the deck of a wooden ship. And it was sinking! The water washed over the side of the boat and left us sitting on the deck. Just as I tried standing up, another stinging wave crashed on top of us. Now I was face down on the deck. I heard the scared angry guy shouting again. **"Kill them now before they escape!"**

I was relieved to see that the shouting man was looking away from us and down inside the ship. A Roman soldier grabbed him by the neck and shouted, "No! Paul must live! If you can swim, jump now before the ship goes under. I'll get the others out."

Many men began to jump off of the ship. I wondered if we should jump, too. I didn't have to wonder long. Another wave crashed down over us. This time it pulled us into the sea!

No matter how scared you are, you can't scream when you are trying to survive being thrown over a ship. And believe me, when you're flailing around the water next to a sinking ship, you want to scream! Everything was gray and bubbly and choppy in the water. I could see legs and arms splashing around me. I kicked my legs like crazy but didn't seem to go anywhere.

Finally I saw a hand reach down. It grabbed my hand and pulled me up. I found myself clinging to a floating piece of the wrecked ship. The man who pulled me up was clinging to the wood with me. I tried to thank him, but instead of words, water came out. I coughed about half a gallon of water out of my lungs.

Where were Molly and Ginny? I yelled, "God!"

The man next to me on the wreckage said, "The Father has already answered your prayer. An angel of the Lord has told me that not one life will be lost in this wreck. Look." He pointed toward the sinking ship. Stripe was swimming hard for a broken door that was floating away from the shipwreck. Molly was holding tight to his collar.

"And there is your other friend," the man said. He pointed in the opposite direction. There was an island in the distance. I could see Ginny swimming toward the land. We were all okay. "You are in the care of the living God," he said. "You will live another day."

Sure enough, we all landed on a sandy beach. I've never been so happy to see dry land. I was even happier to see my pesky sister. She was lying on her back. Her chest moved up and down rapidly. Stripe was sitting tall next to her like a guard dog.

"Are you okay?" It was Ginny. In between deep breaths I told her I was all right. She said, "I know where we are. Do you know who it is that saved you?

"No," I answered. "Who?"

"That was Paul. As in Saint Paul. A lot of the book of Acts is about him. He was a prisoner on that ship."

"Is that who those guys wanted to kill?" I asked.

"I think so. They might have been worried that Paul and the other prisoners were going to escape."

"Paul was a good guy," I said. "Why would he be a prisoner?"

"He was under arrest a lot of the time because back then . . . I think it was because he wasn't supposed to tell people about Jesus."

By now Molly and Stripe had come over to us. Molly's voice was weak. "I don't think I want any more *adventure*."

I put my arm around her shoulders. "We're going to be okay now, Sis."

Paul was asking all the people on the beach if they were okay. Another person had started a fire on the beach. Paul invited us to get close to it so we could dry off and warm up. Once everyone moved near the fire he went to the woods at the edge of the beach and picked up firewood. He was bending over to pick up a hunk of wood when he stood up real quick.

Molly said, "Look! There's a stick hanging off his hand!"

"That's not a stick," Ginny said.

I finished for her, "It's a snake!"

Paul held his hand in front of his face. He stared at the snake for a few seconds like he was admiring the pattern in its scales. The snake hung on tight.

Some of the guys next to us began to whisper frantically at each other. "That snake bit his hand!"

"He'll be dead soon!" another said.

I shouted, "Someone help him!"

Paul flung his hand hard and the snake came off. Then Paul just kept picking up firewood like nothing had happened. He stacked the wood by to the fire and sat next to us. "Are you children warm enough?"

I couldn't believe what I was seeing. "Aren't you worried?"

"Yes," he said. "That is why I asked how you're doing."

"No," I replied, "aren't you worried about your snakebite? Aren't you worried about dying?"

He looked at his hand and smiled. "No. I'm not scared. Live or die, I belong to the living God. Jesus

Christ has defeated death with his resurrection. If I die I will be with God. If I am alive I am able to tell people about God's grace and forgiveness. Life with our God is always on the edge. But I am never afraid. God is with me." He looked at his hand again. He looked up at the woods. "And God is with you, too." He pointed. Travel Fish was waiting for us.

"Thanks, Mr. Paul," my sister said.

We climbed into Travel Fish. The first thing I did was admit to Voice of Travel Fish, "Okay, there is adventure in the Bible. I think I've had enough for today."

Molly usually races to be the one who pushes the buttons in Travel Fish. I'm a lot bigger than she is, but once she knocked me over to get to the button. Now she just lay on her chair like she was made of putty. "You do it," she moaned.

I reached up and pushed the button.

The juicy robot burp surrounded us.

My earlobes and nose hairs might have tingled. I might have smelled the smell of sour apple gummy worms. I was too tired to notice.

How to Be Free Instead of a Slave

Some Ways that Everyone Is a Slave

We are captive to:
Sin
Fear
Death

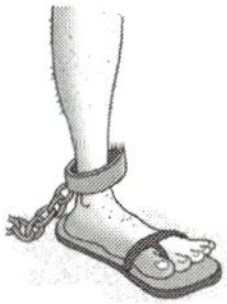

Jesus wins over all the things that lock us up.

What are the parts of my Bible?

Letters:

Romans—Revelation

Pronunciation Key

Onesimus
o – NES – i – mus

Philemon
phil – E – mon

This is Philemon. He is looking for Onesimus. You'll see why when you read the next page.

Philemon is not the shortest book in the Bible but it is only one chapter long!

Step 1: Run Away

Onesimus took money from his master Philemon, probably to pay for travel. (Philemon 1:18)

Step 5: Go Back

Return to the one who used to own you to show your freedom.

Paul was asking Philemon to be a reflection of Christ. Reflection means to be like—or act like—someone.

Step 3: Learn about Jesus

Paul wrote Ephesians, Philippians, Colossians, and Philemon when he was in prison. They were letters to churches and to individuals. Somehow, Onesimus met Paul during this prison story.

Step 4: Be Free in Christ

Paul wrote a plea to Philemon. Then he gave the letter to Onesimus to deliver to Philemon. Here are some things he said in his letter:

Step 2: Go on the Lam

In this case, "on the lam" means hiding from the authorities, not standing on an actual lamb.

Other Bible people who spent time on the lam:
Moses (Exodus 2:11-15)
Elijah (1 Kings 19:1-13)
David (1 Samuel 21:10)
Jesus, Mary, and Joseph (Matthew 2:13-14)

Please help Onesimus. He is a good friend and like a son to me. I wish he could stay here with me to help preach the good news. But now he is returning to you. I hope you will welcome him back as you would welcome me back—as a brother, free in Christ! If he owes you anything, I promise to pay you back.

Parallel Timelines

Before 4000 B.C.—Creation, Adam, and Eve

Around 2400 B.C.—The Ark and the Flood

Around 2100 B.C.—God chooses Abraham

Around 2000 B.C.—Jacob and Esau

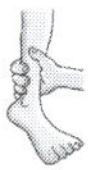

1526 B.C.—Moses born

Around 1440 B.C.—The Plagues

1010 B.C.—King David

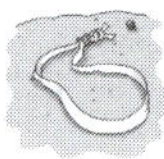

Around 4500 B.C.—First sailing ships

Around 3000 B.C.—Horses domesticated

Around 3000 B.C.—Hieroglyphic writing invented

Around 3000 B.C.—Oil lamps invented

Around 2500 B.C.—Sphinx

Around 2500 B.C.—Pyramids

What are the parts of my Bible?

Old Testament and New Testament

Bible

600 B.C.—Shadrach, Merschach, and Abednego

Around 536 B.C.—Daniel

About 3 B.C.—Jesus is born

30 A.D.—Jesus is crucified and resurrected from the dead

31 A.D.—The coming of the Holy Spirit at Pentecost, the birthday of the church

64 A.D.—Rome burns and Nero blames the Christians

Other World History

Around 1440 B.C.—Iron used for swords and other weapons

Around 1330-1320 B.C.—The reign of King Tut

776 B.C.—First Olympics

400 B.C.—Kites and catapults

Around 300-150 B.C.—Gunpowder invented in China

Holy Spirit, Comfy Spirit

Who is the Holy Spirit?

The Holy Spirit is the Comforter

Travel Fish is pretty cool. It has taken us on *adventures* and to scary places in the Bible. It has been awesome to meet people in the Bible. It is almost always exciting.

There was this one not-so-exciting time though. Ginny wanted to visit John 14. It was kind of boring. Don't get me wrong—Jesus was there and it's always cool to see him and be with him. But he wasn't chasing demons or bringing dead people back to life or calming storms or anything. He was just talking.

Ginny really liked it. She has a better brain for that kind of stuff than I do. Molly and Stripe ran off and played with some kids who were there. I tried hard to pay attention to Jesus. I guess it was sort of like he was giving the disciples some instructions. He told them that when he was gone he would send the Comforter to be with them.

I leaned over to Ginny and whispered, "I don't get it. Why would he call the Holy Spirit a blanket?"

"Shhh!" she scolded me.

I sighed and stared at the cracks it the wall. When Jesus was done talking we called for Molly and Stripe and we all got back into Travel Fish. Molly pushed the button to get us back home.

My nose hairs and my earlobes were all tingly, and I smelled the smell of sour apple gummy worms. The juicy robot belch was fading.

Ginny looked crabby and she opened her mouth to say something to me but Molly interrupted, "Hey! Let's go out and play ARCHAEOLOGIST. We can pretend we're digging for David's slingshot or Goliath's helmet. No, wait! We'll pretend we're looking for Goliath's skull!"

One of our favorite things to do at the empty lot where we play is to pretend we're archaeologists digging for artifacts. Now that we have Travel Fish, we always pretend to be looking for artifacts from the Bible. We got the shovels that we keep hidden in the pile of old tires and started digging.

I turned to Ginny. She still looked cranky so I asked her, "Why are you so crabby?"

Her answer was right on the tip of her tongue, "We

were listening to Jesus! You kept whispering at me. Why can't you pay attention?"

"I was trying to pay attention! All I said was that I didn't understand what he meant."

"I don't understand how you can't understand," she said.

"Oh yeah? Well I can't understand how you can't understand that I can't understand!"

Molly stopped digging and looked at us, "Yikes! You guys sound like you're brother and sister or something."

Ginny dropped her shovel and went home in a huff.

That was Sunday.

Before I tell you about Monday I have to tell you a secret. I am scared of thunderstorms. I am very scared of thunderstorms. I am double extra very scared of thunderstorms. Up until now I was the only person who knew this so don't go blabbing it around.

You also need to know that this year my folks decided I am big enough to be alone for a little bit after school. So on Mondays and Fridays I am alone for about two hours until Mom and Dad get home from work. Those are the days when Molly goes to her day care after kindergarten. Yep, it's just me and Stripe.

These are the rules for being home alone: 1. Lock the doors. 2. Don't answer the phone. 3. Don't go on the

Internet. 4. Don't let anyone in the house (friends or strangers).

What's cool about being home alone is I get to watch any TV show I want without Molly hogging it. Oh, another cool thing is that I have an extra cookie for my after school snack. (That's another secret. Don't tell anyone, all right?)

So on Monday I got home. I let Stripe outside to pee and then locked the doors tight. So far, so good. I was on my second cookie when I heard it—a rumble off in the distance. I tried to convince myself that it was just a train going past or that it was a giant lake monster rampaging through town. But I wasn't that lucky.

Another rumble growled in my ear, **"It's not a train, Johnny."**

There was a flash of lightning before the next rumble. **"I'm definitely a thunderstorm, Johnny. And did you notice that you're home alone? Shouldn't you be scared?"**

The thunder was right. I was about as scared as I'd ever been. I ran through the house and turned on every light. I turned the TV to the weather channel and got all my Thermo Man comic books and piled them in the center of the living room. I was too scared to read, though. I just looked at the pictures, closing my eyes tight whenever the thunder howled and yelled at me.

The rain sounded like a thousand gremlins running around on the roof of our house. The wind slapped a tree branch up against the living room windows. I was so scared! I can't even think of enough words to tell you how bad it was.

I looked at my watch. Another hour and a half until anyone else gets home! I thought I would probably be the first person to die of thunderstorm fright.

I started imagining what it would be like when Mom and Dad got home and found my lifeless body. Boy, my folks will be sorry they ever thought I was big enough to be home alone. They would come home and find me lying on the circle rug of our living room, covered in Thermo Man comics with my tongue hanging out. And they'd get down on their knees and cry, "Oh Johnny! We're so sorry! How could we have been so wrong?"

My kid sister would probably yell, "Cool! Can I have his room?"

I was starting to wonder who would be at my funeral when the front door opened. "Hey, kiddo!" I have never been so happy to see my dad get home.

He said, "I heard the storm coming so I left work early so you wouldn't have to be here alone."

"Oh . . . that's okay," I said. "You didn't have to do that. But thanks anyway."

"You want to go out to the porch and watch the storm?" he asked.

"Sure," I said, like it was the best idea I'd ever heard.

Dad and I went out to our big, screened-in porch in the back of our house. He put his arm around me as we watched the storm.

Lightning cracked right outside the porch and lit up the dark sky brighter than the sun. The thunder that followed was so loud that I could feel it in the floor and in my chest.

"Whoa! That was a good one," said Dad.

"Yeah, cool," I agreed. And I really did agree with him, too.

We sat there and watched the rest of the storm. By the time Mom and Molly got home, the show was over.

At bedtime I climbed in under my blankets and pulled out my walkie-talkie from the nightstand. The other walkie-talkie was at Ginny's house next door. We often talked on them at bedtime.

I clicked the talk button, "Come in, Ginny, this is Johnny, over."

Silence.

I worried that maybe she had hers turned off because she was still mad at me.

"Come in, Ginny. Are you there?"

My walkie talkie crackled, "I'm here," she said. "That was some storm, huh?"

"You can say that again," I answered.

She said it again, "That was some storm, huh?"

"Hardy, har, har," I fake laughed. "Listen, the storm taught me something."

"What?" she asked.

I told her, "I get what Jesus meant by calling the Holy Spirit the Comforter. I was home alone when the storm started."

"Were you scared?"

"Sort of," I fibbed. "Well . . . actually I was scared a lot. But then my dad got home and we watched the storm together from the porch. I was right in the middle of the storm and I felt safe. My dad comforted me. The storm was still going on but it was like it didn't matter as long as he was there next to me."

"That's it," she said. "Jesus knew he wasn't going to be there right next to the disciples. He knew things would get scary and rough for them. So he told them that the Holy Spirit would be with them to take care of them. There are all kinds of places in the Bible where the disciples are in jail or some kind of trouble but they are not scared. They were being comforted by the Holy Spirit."

"Cool," I said. "Do you think the Holy Spirit is still around?"

"Sure," she answered. "Jesus didn't put a time limit on it. It's a scary world, and we still need comfort. Mom says our church teaches and believes that the Holy Spirit is part of us today, too."

"Well," I said, I'm glad I finally got it."

"Me, too," she replied. "And Johnny . . ."

"What?"

"I'm sorry I got so mad at you."

"That's all right," I said.

"No, really," she continued, "we don't have to understand all the same stuff all at the same time. I really am sorry."

"Okay, okay," I said. "You're forgiven." I heard some new thunder in the distance. "Did you hear that?"

"Yeah. I think another storm is coming," answered Ginny.

"Good night," I said. "I've got to get my comforter for bedtime."

Chicken Fight Church

Who is the Holy Spirit?

The Holy Spirit gives birth to the Church

I heard my Uncle Jimmy arguing with my dad about church once. He said he doesn't go to church because he doesn't like "organized religion." I'm not sure if I know exactly what he meant, but if he doesn't like organized religion he probably would have loved to be there at Pentecost, the time when the church was born.

It didn't look organized at all. It was crazy and wild! I know because I was there. It's not like I'm 2,000 years old or something. Travel Fish took me, Ginny, Molly, and Stripe to chapter 2 in the book of Acts.

In our adventures with Travel Fish we made friends with Bartholomew, one of Jesus' disciples. None of us could pronounce his name so we just call him Bart. He always seems to know when we are coming. He was there waiting for us when Travel Fish dropped us off at Acts 2.

He looked scared. "Come quickly," he whispered. As we followed him out into the street he told us, "We are not popular with the authorities. They are still mad at us because we worship Jesus. They thought they killed him. But he rose again."

"Hey, I knew that!" Molly exclaimed. "I learned that in Sunday school!"

Bart managed a smile. "Very good, child. Today we must meet secretly to worship Jesus."

The streets were jam packed with people. It was difficult to make our way through. Bart said that Jews from all over were gathered here in Jerusalem for a very important religious celebration. They shared the same religion but they spoke many different languages.

He led us into a small building. The room they were sitting in was dark and cramped. The disciples were quietly telling each other about things Jesus had said and done when he was with them. One of them said, "Those were good days. I want Jesus back with us."

"Don't forget," Peter said, "our Lord told us that the Holy Spirit will come to us. We will not have fear then. We will have God's power."

We all heard a far away rumbling. Somebody jumped up and peeked out a window. "Are they coming to get us?" asked a frightened apostle.

Before anyone could answer him a huge wind blasted into the room. It sounded like a train and a tornado wrapped into one crazy bundle. Cups blew off the table.

Everybody's hair was blowing like crazy. Dust whirled around us like cars on a racetrack.

Just when I thought it couldn't have gotten any louder, it did. Out of nowhere a flock of flames roared into the room. They swirled around the same race track as the dust. Disciples were staring at the flames like they couldn't believe what was happening.

Ginny shouted to Bart, "What's happening?"

"I don't know," he hollered back. He pushed the three of us behind him to keep us out of danger.

Finally the wind and fire slowed down. The room began to get quiet again. No one said a word as the apostles began to look around. The wind was gone and the fire was silent now. But get this—there were twelve disciples and each one had a flame dancing over his head!

Someone finally opened his mouth to speak but I couldn't understand a thing he said. Nobody else could either. Everybody looked at him like he was purple or something. Someone else began speaking in another different language. One more did the same. Finally each one of them was speaking. Twelve disciples—twelve different languages. It sounded like a chicken fight in that room.

Peter finally stood up on the table and motioned for the others to follow him outside. All at once they understood what he wanted. We followed them out of the house and saw that a crowd had gathered.

"So much for the disciples hiding out," Ginny said.

The crowd had heard the racket and were curious about what was happening. Peter was the first one to speak in some strange new language. Some of the crowd seemed to understand him. They gathered around to listen. Then, one by one, each of the disciples began to speak. Each of them had his own crowd of listeners. It went on like this for quite a while until Bart finally came back to us.

He looked like a kid who just got everything he wanted for Christmas. "This is the Spirit and power that Jesus promised!" he said. "This is something new. This is the church. We are telling all these people about Jesus. We are telling them that he is God's Son and that he loves them. This is what we are supposed to do. We won't hide anymore. We will tell everyone we see that Jesus is God!"

He took off in a FLASH and found another group of people to talk to about Jesus.

So that was the beginning of the Christian church. There was a lot of wind, fire, noise, confusion, and fear. There was nothing organized about it at all. But, as Voice of Travel Fish pointed out, it was still God who was in charge.

We found our way back to Travel Fish and it burped us back home. As usual Stripe was the first one to jump out. He went straight toward the big brown tabby cat that usually hangs out at the empty lot. Chasing that thing is one his favorite sports. I am 99 percent certain that this time, instead of barking at the cat, Stripe meowed at it.

My Cousin, the Son of God

Who is the Holy Spirit?

The Holy Spirit is present at Jesus' baptism

Some similarities and differences between Jesus and John the Baptizer

John ate locusts and honey (Mark 1:6).

Jesus ate the same food as others (John 21:10-14).

Jesus wore the same kind of clothes as other people. John wore camel hair with a leather belt around his waist (Mark 1:6).

John baptized Jes
in the Jordan Riv
Then a bird car
down from the s
The Holy Spirit w
at the baptism
Jesus (Matthew
Mark 1:10). The pr
ence of the Ho
Spirit showed th
Jesus was doi

The angel Gabriel announced to Mary, a young virgin, that she would be mother to Jesus (Luke 1:26). Jesus was born to Mary by the power of the Holy Spirit.

The angel Gabriel announced to Zechariah that John would be born (Luke 1:12). John's parents, Zechariah and Elizabeth, were old (Luke 1:18-20).

od's work, that
sus is God's son,
nd that Jesus is
od. When someone
baptized today,
ey usually hear the
ords "*Child of God,*
u have been sealed
the Holy Spirit and
arked with the cross
Christ forever."

Jesus had disciples. Jesus has disciples today! (You are one!)

John had disciples. John does not have disciples today.

Disciple: someone who follows and learns from a teacher

How to Make a Paper Airplane, a Palm Tree, a Peanut Butter & Jelly Sandwich, and a Disciple

Who is the Holy Spirit?

The Holy Spirit is present at the Great Commission

How to Make a Paper Airplane

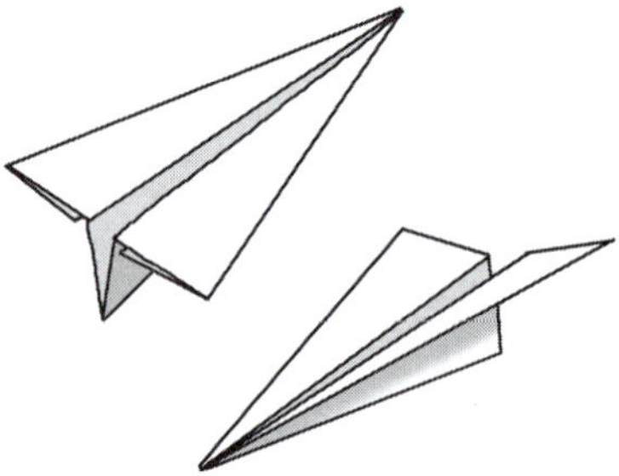

I learned this from my grandpa.

You'll need a piece of paper. The kind in your computer printer is good for this. Fold it in half the long way.

Fold one of the top corners down so that the edge meets the fold. Flip it over and do the same thing with the other top corner.

Fold down the top edge on each side again, making the edges meet each other at the first fold.

Fold them one more time.

Now throw it.

How to Make a Palm Tree Using a Green Pepper and a Carrot (the most fun a kid can have with vegetables)

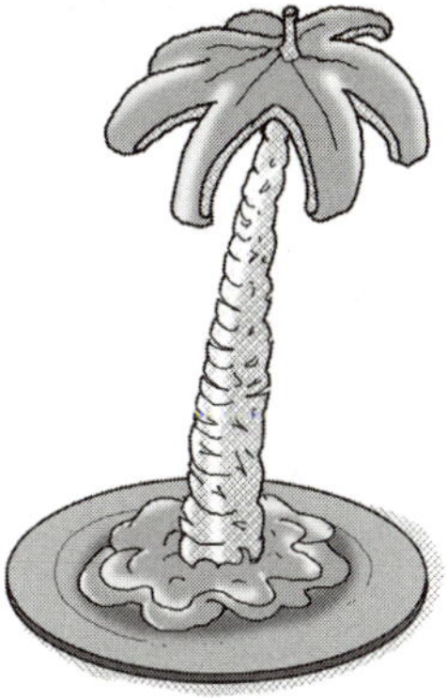

I learned this one from my dad.

You'll need a carrot, a green pepper, a knife, and a cutting board. You will also need a grown-up to make sure you don't run around with the knife or cut the tip of your finger off and bleed all over the kitchen or something.

Slice a bit of the big end and the pointy end off of a carrot.

Cut a green pepper so it looks like palms on a palm tree.

Make little bitty slices on the edge of the carrot to look like palm tree bark.

You can use a glop of peanut butter to make the palms (pepper) stick on top of the trunk (carrot). (If you're like my friend Melvin Noy and you are allergic to peanut butter, you can use soy butter instead.)

Put a glop of peanut butter on a plate. Stick the palm tree in the glop of peanut butter.

Remember—even though you could eat the mini palm tree, don't. This is a garnish which means it is art done with food to make the food you're actually going to eat look special.

How to Make a Peanut Butter & Jelly Sandwich

I learned this one from my mom.

You'll need peanut butter, your favorite color of jelly, two pieces of bread, a butter knife, and a plate. (And remember, if you are allergic to peanut butter, use another kind of spread.) You'll need permission, but you probably won't need adult supervision since it's very tough to cut anything off with a butter knife. But you'd better let your parents or somebody grown up decide if you need supervision.

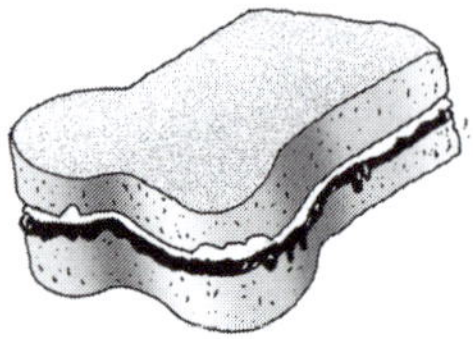

Lay the bread on the plate.

Spread peanut butter on one slice of bread. (I like to put the peanut butter on really thick.)

Spread jelly on the other slice of bread. (If you're like my best friend Ginny you will want more jelly than peanut butter.)

Put the two pieces of bread together so that the peanut butter and jelly face each other on the inside.

You get extra points if the peanut butter and jelly ooze over the crust. But be sure to eat it over the plate so that you don't drip it on the floor (especially the carpet) and get hollered at. I know this from personal experience.

I let my dog Stripe lick the butter knife. Mom, if you're reading this, I have *never* put the knife back in the drawer ever since the one time I did that.

Clean up after yourself. Put stuff away.

My sister likes to put a slice of jalapeño cheese in the center. I think it's nasty but she wouldn't leave me alone until I put it in these instructions.

How to Make a Disciple

Disciple is another word for "Christian." Disciples aren't just those 12 guys in the Bible. Disciples are people who believe in Jesus and belong to Jesus. Disciples are people who keep learning from Jesus and who help take care of people the way Jesus takes care of people.

I learned this from God, who used the Holy Spirit, the Bible, and Travel Fish to teach Molly, Ginny, and me. We were at Matthew 28:19-20. It was awesome because this was after Jesus died on the cross and after he rose again. (That was called the resurrection). He was giving his last instructions to the disciples. He was getting them ready to be his people even though they wouldn't be able to see him in person anymore.

You'll need God's word,* water▲, faith,◆ a person to get baptized, and a person to do the baptizing.❖

The person being baptized should be near the water. A lot of churches use a **font,** which is like a fancy water bowl. The person stands next to it. (If the person is a baby and can't stand yet, someone holds the baby.) Some other churches use a little pool and the person gets into it. The rest of my instructions will be for a font.

If it's an older kid or a grown up, they need to bend over so their head is above the water. If it's a baby, someone who loves the baby and won't drop it should hold it over the font. For the rest of my instructions let's say it's a baby named Jerry.

Another person[*] pours water on Jerry's head and says, "Jerry, you are baptized in the name of the Father . . ."

Then they put more water on Jerry's little head and say, "and of the Son . . ."

Then they put one last splash of water on Jerry's head and say, "and of the Holy Spirit."

Then Jerry spends the whole rest of his life learning about Jesus and believing Jesus and loving like Jesus.

That's how you make a disciple.

Pastor Stayput taught us that baptism is more than a symbol. "Baptism does something," she said. And she told us about Romans 6:3-9 where it says baptism connects us to Jesus' death, which is kinda scary. But it also connects us to Jesus' resurrection, which is cool. She taught us that baptism is for forgiveness and it makes us part of God's family.

* God's word for baptism is, ". . . in the name of the Father, Son, and Holy Spirit," from Matthew 28:19.

▲ It's not magic water or anything. It can come from any faucet, even the faucet used to make coffee and lemonade for after church. It's God's word that makes baptism work.

◆ We get our faith from the Holy Spirit. The Holy Spirit helps us believe in the stuff that God promises.

❖ Usually the pastor does the baptism. But Ginny's mom, Pastor Stayput, told us that pastors are not magic and don't zap the baby or have special powers or anything like that. It's God's word that makes it work.

Major Malfunction

Who is the Holy Spirit?

The Holy Spirit leads and guides us to serve

One of the double extra cool things about Travel Fish is finding unbelievably wild Bible passages and going to see them with our own eyes. Let's say you read about the guy who lived in a cemetery and always chased people away. Sounds creepy, right? Not only could you go see it for yourself but you'd also get to be there when Jesus fixes him up and he becomes a preacher.

Or what if you read about Jonah in the belly of the great fish and you wanted to be there when the fish regurgitated Jonah onto the beach? (*Regurgitated* means spit up, which is a much more polite way to say puked.) Well, you could go to that passage and sit back and wait until you saw the fish swim close to the beach. You would see the big fish open its big mouth and POW there's a prophet sprawled in the sand right in front of you.

That's exactly what I wanted to do but didn't get to because of Travel Fish's big malfunction. It took me a while to convince my kid sister Molly and my best friend Ginny to come along with me. (Remember, the number-one rule about time travel through the Bible is **Never go alone.)** I didn't have to convince my dog Stripe at all. He's always ready for a Travel Fish trip no matter how gross or scary it might get.

I set the dials for Jonah 2:10. Molly reached up to push the purple button that *should have* put us right on the beach where Jonah got regurgitated, but Ginny stopped her. "Are you sure you got the chapter and verse right, Johnny? 'Cause if you didn't we could end up in the stinky belly of the fish. I'll go to the beach with you but the belly would be way too icky."

"I double checked it and triple checked it, Ginny," I huffed at her. I used to be not so good at finding my way around the Bible. But all the practice I got with Travel Fish has really helped. "Go ahead, Molly," I said. "Push it."

She pushed the purple button. Now, normally we would hear a long, loud robot burp. Then our ear hairs and nose hairs would tingle and we would smell the smell of sour apple gummy worms.

But there was a new sound today, and it didn't sound good.

Brrraa

ink ink tingy putt.

The tips of my fingernails tingled, and I smelled the smell of boiled cauliflower.

Voice of Travel Fish chimed in, "Oh dear. There seems to be a malfunction."

"A malfunction?" we all hollered.

"You don't need to worry, children. Travel Fish has a built in program for self-correction. However, this may take some time," explained VTF.

"We could just go home and watch *The Mangles* on TV," offered Molly. "We'll come back to Travel Fish later."

"I'm afraid that won't be possible," said VTF.

"What do you mean it won't be possible? Aren't we at home?" I asked.

"Hey," added Ginny, "how come the door hasn't opened yet? Are we inside Jonah's fish? Are we stuck inside here?" She sounded scared, which is not like Ginny at all.

"You need not worry, children," VTF assured us. "You are safe. Travel Fish has sent you to an alternate passage. When the door does open you will be in Jerusalem during the time of Jesus. However, you are in-between passages. Jesus himself is currently in another city, healing a man possessed by demons."

Molly said, "Cool!"

VTF continued, "Not only will this take some time, but Travel Fish has informed me that you must leave while it corrects the verse drive."

The side door opened, filling the cockpit with light and smells and sounds from the busy streets of

Jerusalem. "Well," said VTF, trying to sound hopeful, "let's go exploring."

We slowly climbed out of Travel Fish. I was nervous because there is usually a person from the Bible ready to meet us and show us around. "We're all on our own," I said.

"No need to fret," said VTF. "I am equipped with maps of ancient Jerusalem. We only have a 3.7 percent chance of getting lost. Let's explore. Travel Fish will contact me when the repairs are complete."

"C'mon," urged Molly. "Ol' VTF has never let us down before."

We began walking down the street. Up and down the street were booths where merchants were selling all kinds of interesting food and clothing and chickens in cages.

A fat man in a bright green outfit held one of the chickens and asked the merchant, "Does this hen lay good eggs?"

"She's my best egg layer," answered the merchant.

A gaggle of little kids ran past us, weaving their way in and out of the grown-ups who filled the street.

Ginny whispered nervously, "I'm still not sure about this. What if we get stuck here or something?" The little kids were running back toward us. The last one must have just learned to run, he looked so little. He's the one who banged into Molly and fell to the ground. He sat up and looked at his bloody knees and started bawling instantly.

Ginny planted her fists on her hips and scolded him, "Watch where you're going, kid!" The child got up and limped away, crying and holding his knees.

"He could've really hurt me," griped Molly.

We continued down the street. "Travel Fish better get fixed quick, and I better not miss my chance to see Jonah get spit up into the sand," I grumbled. "This place is kinda boring."

We passed a lady in raggedy clothes sitting right in the middle of the street. Stripe and I walked around her left side. Molly and Ginny went around her right. I was saying, "Boy, am I starving! I could go for some **CHOCO-CREAMY-PUFFERS**." I dug in my pockets, "Yuck! All I've got are almonds."

The raggedy lady in the middle of the street held her empty hand up to me. I popped an almond into my mouth and asked the girls, "Did you see how filthy that lady's hands were? Eww." Stripe looked back at her and whimpered.

Molly said, "I'm pretty sure I'm going to miss *The Mangles.* Today was supposed to be the episode where they sing their way to the North Pole. Now that Travel Fish is busted I'll never get to see it."

A little further down the street we heard a man calling out, "Alms! Alms for the blind!" He was kneeling in the doorway of a building. A small basket with a few coins was in front of him. We saw a big burly guy come out of the crowd and kick the basket away from the blind guy. "You'd better go look for your money, old man!" he teased.

Burly Guy walked away and Blind Guy began crawling out in the street, feeling for his coins. "Yeesh," said Molly, "he'll never find that money."

Stripe began sniffing the ground next to the blind man. "Let's get going, Stripe," I ordered.

From Ginny's front pocket we heard VTF chime. Ginny pulled her out and VTF said, "Travel Fish is ready for you to come back."

We raced back past the blind guy who was still looking for his coins. The raggedy lady in the middle of the road still had her dirty hand out as we zipped around her. When we spotted Travel Fish waiting for us we also saw the little boy with bloody knees. He was all alone now and crying for his momma.

We passed around him and jumped into Travel Fish.

"It's about time," I griped. "Let's go to the beach and see a big sick fish!"

Molly reached for the purple button.

Brrraa

ink ink tingy putt.

The tips of my fingernails tingled, and I smelled the smell of boiled cauliflower.

Voice of Travel Fish chimed in, "Oh dear, there still seems to be a malfunction."

"Another malfunction?" we all hollered.

"You don't need to worry, children. We are still at the alternate passage. We will have to step out again," explained VTF.

VTF continued, "Not only will this take some time, but Travel Fish has informed me that you must leave while it corrects the verse drive."

Then the side door opened, filling the cockpit with light and smells and sounds from the busy streets of Jerusalem. "Well," said VTF, trying to sound hopeful, "let's go exploring."

We began walking down the street. Up and down the street were booths where merchants were selling all kinds of interesting food and clothing and chickens in cages.

A fat man in a bright green outfit held one of the chickens and asked the merchant, "Does this hen lay good eggs?"

"She's my best egg layer," answered the merchant.

A gaggle of little kids ran past us, weaving their way in and out of the grown-ups who filled the street.

Ginny whispered, "Wait a second! Those are exactly the same people saying exactly the same things they said the first time we saw them. Voice, what's going on?"

VTF answered, "It's quite normal. When Travel Fish malfunctioned the second time it brought us back to the same spot in time as before. You will be seeing and experiencing all the same sights and sounds as before."

The little kids were running back toward us. The last one must have just learned to run, he looked so little. He's the one who banged into Molly and fell to the ground. He sat up and looked at his bloody knees and started bawling instantly.

Ginny knelt down to him and said, "Oh! I'm sorry little guy." As she helped him up, she spotted the blood on his knees.

While she was comforting him and wiping the blood with the edge of her sleeve Molly called out to the little boy's friends, "Hey! You guys lost one!" The kids came back and scooped up the boy and led him away.

We passed a lady in raggedy clothes sitting right in the middle of the street. We stopped in front of her. Ginny asked, "Are you okay, ma'am?" The raggedy woman just groaned. "Here," Ginny offered, "let's get you out of the middle of the street before you get hurt."

We helped her off the street. She held out her hands. Molly asked her, "Are you hungry?" The lady held her hands out farther.

"Here," I said, "I've got some almonds you can have." I dug them out of my pocket and gave them to her.

"Bless you," she said and began eating them.

"You're welcome," we said as we walked away.

A little further down the street we heard a man calling out, "Alms! Alms for the blind!" He was kneeling

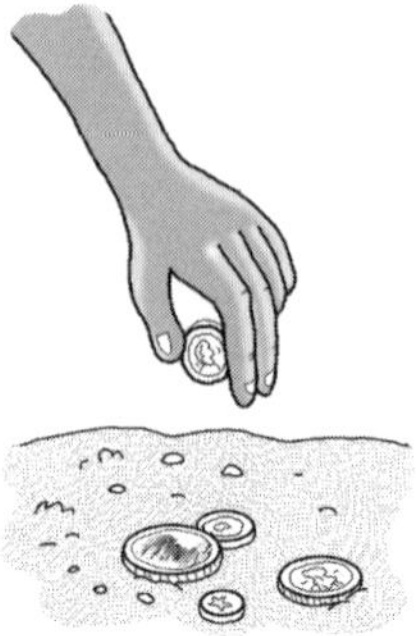

in the doorway of a building. A small basket with a few coins was in front of him. We saw a big burly guy come out of the crowd and kick the basket away from the blind guy. "You'd better go look for your money, old man!" he teased.

Burly Guy walked away and Blind Guy began crawling out in the street, feeling for his coins. Stripe began sniffing the ground next to the blind man. Molly got down and joined him. Ginny and I both spotted coins across the street and picked them up. We found all the coins and helped him back to the doorway.

"Will you be okay here?" Ginny asked.

"Bless you, my children," he said.

From Ginny's front pocket we heard VTF chime. Ginny pulled her out, and VTF said, "Travel Fish is ready for you to come back."

We raced back to Travel Fish and dove into the cockpit one more time.

"Who's ready for the beach?" I yelled.

VTF said, "Wait, children. I told you things would be the same but things were quite different this time. Did you notice?"

We looked at each other kind of confused and then all three of us shook our heads. "No," Ginny said.

I added, "There was the guy buying a hen; the same smells; and the kid bumping into Molly."

"Oh!" said Molly, "There was the hungry lady and the blind guy and the bully, too. We shoulda kicked him in the knee or something."

VTF spoke up again, "You certainly did see the same things. But you were different."

We looked at each other some more. Finally Ginny yelled, "Yes! The first time we complained and ignored those people."

"The second time we helped them," I added.

"I have a confession to make, kids," said VTF. "There was no malfunction. Travel Fish was programmed to teach you about the leading of the Holy Spirit."

"Well, what did we learn?" asked Molly.

Voice of Travel Fish told us that the first time we went down the street the Holy Spirit purposefully held back on its job. The second time the Spirit did its job. It led us to help when we saw people in need.

Ginny said, "All we did the first time was complain and worry about ourselves and what we were missing."

"Correct," said VTF, "One of the jobs of the Holy Spirit is to lead disciples to look beyond themselves and to share the goodness of Jesus with other people."

I pointed out that we hadn't said anything about Jesus to those people. But VTF told me that we share Jesus in what we say *and* what we do.

"Cool," said Molly.

Voice of Travel Fish said, "Now who wants to go to the beach?"

Banana Sticks

Why do I serve others?

Because Jesus first served us

"BECAUSE MOM AND DAD SAID SO! THAT'S WHY!" My kid sister Molly was yelling at me, if you can believe that.

But that's okay. I can yell, too. **"They didn't say I had to cut the banana lengthwise!"**

Molly yelled again, "I'M NOT GONNA EAT IT!" She stormed out of the kitchen and into her room. She slammed the door.

You see, every Tuesday I have to babysit Molly after school for about an hour until my dad gets home from work. So I am in charge. Every Tuesday morning before school Mom says, "This afternoon Johnny's in charge. He's the boss when we're gone."

And every time Dad adds, "But that doesn't mean he gets to be mean." Then he pretends to frown at me and he says, "You know what I mean?"

It almost always goes okay on Tuesdays but once in

a while it goes like today. I was being SUPER BROTHER and making Molly her favorite after-school snack, bananas with peanut butter and jelly.

It wasn't good enough for Queen Molly though. I cut the banana into two pieces the long way. Molly likes it split into three pieces lengthwise. It's like three banana sticks. Did you know bananas have three sections? Molly does. "Three sections, one banana," she says. "Just like God. Father, Son, Holy Spirit. Three persons, one God." She learned it in Sunday school.

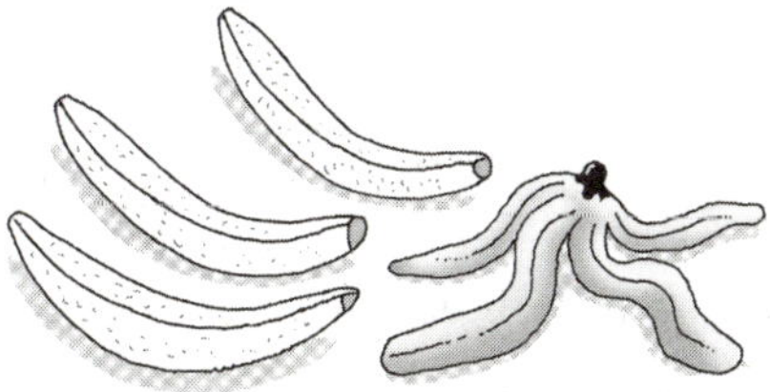

Now she won't eat a banana any other way. "That's the way God made bananas," she says, "so that's the way I'm gonna eat 'em."

The problem is I can't do it. I always end up with a handful of banana mush.

I hollered one more time, "Mom and Dad just said I should make you a snack. They didn't say I had to be your servant and do every little thing you command!"

She opened her door, "You do to have to be my servant. IT'S IN THE BIBLE!"

"Prove it!" I hollered.

Molly came rushing out of her room. "It's in there. We had it in Sunday school this week. Jesus said that people who are the boss of other people are supposed to serve them."

"You're full of baloney," I said.

She put her fists on her hips. "You wanna ask Travel Fish if I'm full of baloney?"

I was pretty sure Jesus wouldn't command me to split a banana into three sections so I said, "Okay, let's go."

Neither of us said a word as we walked to the empty lot and the pile of old tires where Travel Fish hid. Both of us were too mad to talk. Our dog Stripe was the only happy one. He loves Travel Fish.

We climbed into Travel Fish and sat down. Usually Molly jumps right up to the dashboard before anyone else can. She loves to set the dials. This time she just stared at them.

"Well?" I asked like I was offended.

She whined, "I don't remember where it was. But it is in the Bible."

I grabbed Voice of Travel Fish off her hook. VTF is a keychain, but she's really more of a tour guide. She looks like a miniature version of Travel Fish. She goes with us when we travel into the Bible. I asked, "Can Travel Fish take us somewhere in the Bible where Jesus says I have to split a banana in three pieces just because my kid sister says so?"

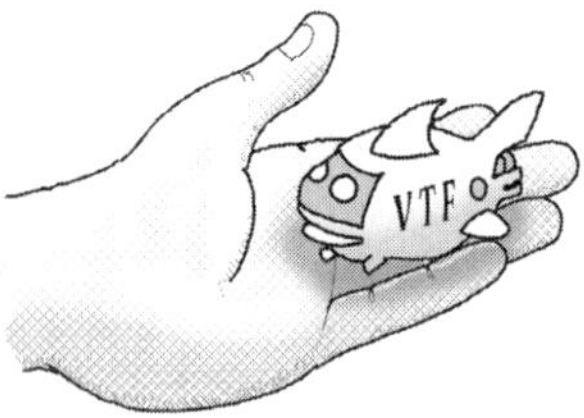

Her calm voice answered, "I don't believe there is a place in Scriptures in which the Lord speaks of bananas."

I sneered at Molly. "See?"

Molly said, "No, I said that Jesus said that people who are the boss of other people are supposed to serve them."

"Why, yes," said VTF, "we can go there. Please set the dials for the Gospel of John 13:1."

"See?" Molly imitated me. She leaned over to the dashboard. **Click, click, click** to the book of John. **Click, click** to chapter 13. **Click, click, click** to verse 1. She pushed the purple button.

My nose hairs and my earlobes were all tingly, and I smelled the smell of sour apple gummy worms. The juicy robot belch faded.

Travel Fish's door opened. It looked like we were in the backyard of some Bible time house. Voice of Travel Fish said, "Please go out to the front of the home. Someone is waiting for you."

Sure enough, at the front of the house was a man with a thick beard and curly black hair. "The Lord be with you," he said.

Molly and I surprised ourselves when we both answered, "And also with you." It was the same thing we say in church sometimes.

"I am Bartholomew."

"Bart-a-who?" Molly asked.

"Bartholomew," he answered.

"Barmazoo?" she asked.

"Bartholomew," he said again.

"Bartaloo?"

"Bar . . . just call me Bart," he finally said.

"Oh, hi there, Bart!" Molly was all cheerful. I rolled my eyes.

"I am supposed to bring you to the upper room," he said.

"Wait a second," I said. "How did you know we were coming?"

"I might be as confused as you," Bart answered. "My Lord, Jesus of Nazareth, sent me to meet you. He is a mystery sometimes. Come with me."

He led us inside and up some stairs. A closed door was at the top. Bart turned and faced us. He whispered, "Today is Passover. It's one of our most important holy days. We share a special meal to remember that our God saved us from slavery in Egypt. The meal is just over and Jesus is doing something very strange."

We crept into the room and stood against a wall to watch what was happening. The only sound in the dim room was water splashing gently. Jesus was crouched at the feet of one of his disciples. He was washing the disciples' feet!

All of the disciples looked confused, especially the guy getting his feet washed.

I whispered to Bart, "What's going on?"

"It's very odd," he said, "and somewhat troubling. Jesus is our Lord and teacher. He is our master. And yet . . ."

Molly interrupted him, "You mean he's the boss of you?"

Bart looked at her sort of funny. "Yes. He is our master. Yet he's treating us as if we are the masters. Washing feet is the job of a servant, not a master."

We watched as Jesus washed the next guy's feet. The room was very quiet. In a way it was comforting. Jesus was caring for them. But in a way it was scary. On his face Jesus looked like he was getting ready for something big.

When Jesus had washed all their feet he stood up and wiped his hands. He said, "Do you know what I have done to you? You call me *Teacher* and *Lord*—and you are right, for that is what I am. So if I, your Lord and Teacher, have washed your feet, you also ought to wash one another's feet. For I have set you an example, that you also should do as I have done to you. Very truly, I tell you, servants are not greater than their master, nor are messengers greater than the one who sent them. If you know these things, you are blessed if you do them."

"It's time to go," Bart said. He bent over and took a scrap of food. He tossed it to Stripe and then scratched him behind the ears. Bart led us down the stairs and out of the house.

We thanked him. We were real quiet when we climbed back into Travel Fish.

Travel Fish took us back to the pile of old tires. As we were walking home I said, "You know what happens next in the Bible, don't you? Jesus is gonna die on the cross for them."

"Oh," she said. "That's a lot harder than washing their feet."

When we got a little closer to home I said, "Yeah, it's tougher than splittin' a banana into three pieces, too."

When we got into the kitchen Stripe ran to his water dish to wash down the treat Bart had tossed him. The banana and jelly sundae was still on the table.

I offered to try to make another one with the banana split into three pieces.

"That's okay, I'll eat this one," she said. "Thanks for making it, Johnny."

"You're welcome." I put the jelly jar away, and Dad walked through the door.

Finish Your Lentils

Why do I serve others?

Because Jesus showed us how by feeding and teaching

The first time we went somewhere in the Bible with Travel Fish it was an accident. After that we always had an idea of where we wanted to go. We would turn the dials to the book, chapter, and verse that we wanted and Travel Fish would take us there.

There was a time when Voice of Travel Fish gave us a suggestion. I think we had planned on going to Noah's ark. Molly had it in her head that she wanted to pet the panda bears. But when we sat down VTF spoke up. "May I make a suggestion for you today, children? I have been informed that a certain occurrence in the Gospel of Matthew will be a great importance to you in the very near future."

"Really?" Ginny asked. I couldn't tell if she was worried or just curious. "What is going to happen?"

"I was only informed that you will need the story soon. More I do not know. But remember David and Daniel and Jonah. You may always trust the Lord to protect you."

"Well . . . ," I stammered, "okay." I don't think I sounded too brave.

Molly wasn't worried at all. "Okay! Where should I click the dials?"

"You may set the dials and buttons for Matthew, chapter 9, verse 9."

Click, click, click, Molly turned the dials and pressed the buttons. She pushed the purple button and the whole place filled up with that juicy robot burp.

My nose hairs and my earlobes were all tingly, and I smelled the smell of sour apple gummy worms. The juicy robot belch was fading.

Out the side door of Travel Fish we could see a house. Not a house like yours or mine but a house like they had in Jesus' day. VTF spoke again. "Please go inside the dwelling."

When we got out of Travel Fish we heard voices coming out of the little house. It sounded like more people than could possibly fit in there! But they didn't sound crowded. They laughed and spoke loudly. Someone was telling a funny story about his donkey refusing to walk. Someone else was saying, "Tickle, tickle, tickle!" in a silly voice. A child was laughing so hard it sounded like he might pee in his pants! And the smell of food floated out with the sounds.

Molly said, "It sounds like fun in there! Do you think they'll mind if we join the party?"

Ginny said, "Well, no one has seemed to mind us yet in any of our Bible trips. They all seem to be expecting us when we show up. We've been able to trust VTF so far. Let's go in."

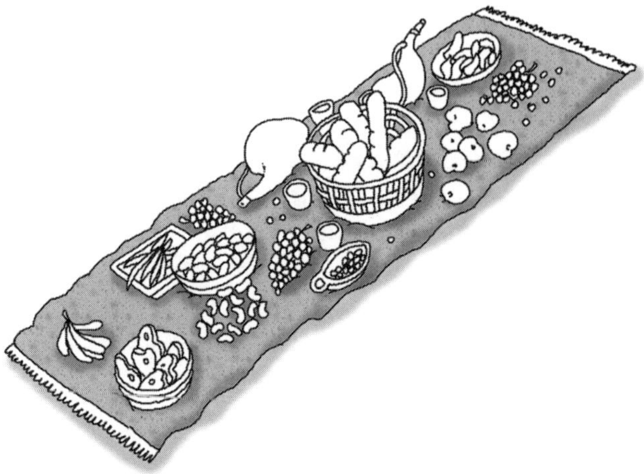

When we peeked in the door we saw many people standing up against the walls. Others were sitting on the floor around a tablecloth that was filled with dishes of food, bread, and cups.

Jesus was there, sitting down by the food. He was listening to a man talk. He looked at us and waved. Then he listened to the man again. We saw Bart on the other side of Jesus. (His real name was Bartholomew but when we met him the first time he told us to call him Bart.) He stood up and came over to us.

"Hello, children! I am pleased to see you and your dog again." Stripe was sitting next to Jesus, begging for food. Jesus ignored the begging. Instead he kept scratching the back of my dog's ears and listening to the man who had been talking to him. Stripe kept his eyes on the food. "Is this a party?" Molly asked. "Whose birthday is it?"

"We are guests here today," said Bart. "Today Jesus brought Matthew into our group." He pointed to the man speaking to Jesus. "Matthew has brought us into his home with many of his friends and family. When we eat it is very much like what you call a party."

Just as Bart finished his sentence the whole house became quiet. I heard Stripe whimper as he ran over to my side. Everyone had stopped talking and were looking at the door where we had just come in. Several men were standing in the doorway. They all looked as if they had just tasted sour milk. One by one they marched in. They were dressed in flowing robes and wore large hats. They worked their way through the crowd until they were standing nose to nose with Bart.

The man who looked the most angry asked, "Why does your teacher eat with tax collectors and sinners?"

Bart opened his mouth to answer, but before any sound came out Jesus was there, and he answered, "It is not the healthy who need a doctor, but the sick. But go and learn what this means: 'I desire mercy, not sacrifice.' For I have not come to call the righteous, but sinners."

After that, those guys looked like they had gotten another mouthful of sour milk. They looked at us and at Stripe and they frowned some more. They stormed out the door. The party started again, as if nothing had happened. Jesus went back and sat by Matthew again.

I asked Bart, "Who were those guys? They gave me the creeps."

"Those were some of the Pharisees. They are a group of religious men who make sure that we all think, act, eat, and live correctly. But they have taken God's commandments and turned them into hundreds of tiny religious rules. What to eat, who to eat with, what pots to use to cook our food."

Ginny wanted to know, "Why were they so mad at Jesus?"

"He is a Rabbi, a religious teacher. And yet he does not obey their rules. Today his offense is that he is eating with sinners and tax collectors. Most people think that these are outcasts. No one wants to be around them. But Jesus is different. He is God's love for all people. But the Pharisees think that a religious teacher like Jesus cannot be close to God and still wish to be with outcasts."

His face got serious and he looked toward Jesus. "I am pleased that our Lord would seek out sinners and outcasts like us. But I fear the Pharisees will use this to harm him.

"But we will stand by him. He gives the love and forgiveness of God to us and to outcasts. Because he gives those things to me, I will do the same for others, especially for the ones that have been left out by the Pharisees."

The party went on around us but we were quiet.

Finally Ginny said, "I think we should go now." I called Stripe. Jesus finally gave him a little piece of food before he ran over to us. We climbed into Travel Fish and Molly pushed the button to go back.

My nose hairs and my earlobes were all tingly, and I smelled the smell of sour apple gummy worms. The juicy robot belch was fading. We were home again.

Travel Fish Artifacts

Why do I serve others?

Because Jesus showed us how by healing and praying

Do you remember me telling you that one of the favorite games that Molly, Ginny, Stripe, and I like to play is ARCHAEOLOGIST? It's a fun game, but we can only pretend to find artifacts, which means we find sticks and pretend they are dinosaur bones. Or we find old junk and pretend it is part of a flying saucer that crashed into the earth a million years ago.

The thing about Travel Fish is that along the way we've been able to come up with some really cool artifacts. There's not enough room here to show you everything so what I've done is given you a partial inventory of stuff that we gathered on our trips. (A "partial inventory" is a list that's not done yet.)

Four stones that David didn't use

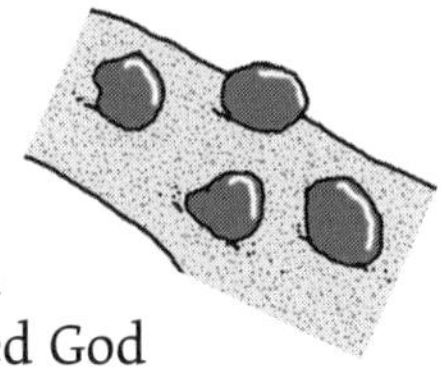

A flower from when Molly and Stripe helped God plant flowers at creation (I pressed it in my Bible)

A couple pieces of straw from the manger where the little Lord Jesus lay down his sweet head

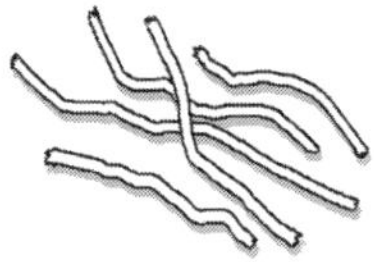

A feather from that same night (I found it on the ground so it might a chicken feather or it might be an angel feather—I'm not sure)

A leg from a locust (this was from John the Baptist's beard)

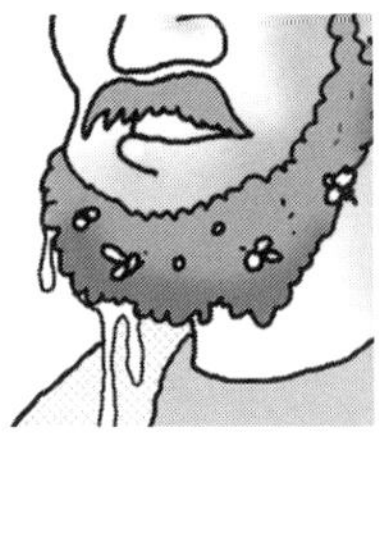

A link of chain from Apostle Paul's chains.

Some hair from Balaam's donkey tail.

A "to-do" list that Jesus kept

TO DO

- Fix sandals
- Pray
- Talk to the guys about who people say that I am
- Heal a blind man (use dirt & spittle this time)
- There is a widow whose only son died—bring him back to life
- Pray for the disciples
- Bring Jairus's daughter back from the dead
- ~~Make up a whole bunch of crabby new rules~~ On second thought, teach people to love God and love each other
- Pray to my Father some more
- Free the guy who lives in the graveyard from demons. Get him washed up. Get him some clothes
- Go to mountain top, pray to Father, visit with Elijah and Moses (bring Peter, James, and John)
- Visit Mom
- Visit Mary, Martha, and Lazarus (Note: Lazarus was dead when I got there so I raised him up)
- Heal at least 10 lepers
- Find large group of people needing healing (blind, lepers, missing or withered hands, etc.) and heal them
- ~~Decide who my favorite people are~~ No. That's silly—I love all people the same!
- I have a feeling Peter will do something rash and harm a Roman soldier. Be prepared to heal the soldier.
- Forgive people who harm me
- Pray . . . ask Father to forgive them, too
- ~~Make people earn my love by being super extra nice~~ That won't fly for one minute—give them my love through healing, praying, and giving myself to them

Did you notice how most of Jesus' "To Do" list was about taking care of people and healing them and stuff? I asked Ginny's mom about that. (Her mom is my pastor.) She said that some folks think Jesus spent most of his time crabbing at people and so now they crab at people. Pastor Stayput said the best way to be like Jesus is to pray for people and take care of them because that's mostly what he did.

S. O. S.

Why do I serve Jesus?

Because people need help

Did you know that you can learn a lot from a keychain? Not just any keychain, though. I'm talking about Voice of Travel Fish. VTF is a keychain shaped exactly like Travel Fish. We take VTF with us whenever we visit a spot in the Bible. She helps us figure out where to go in the Bible. When we are in a Bible passage, she tells us who we are seeing and what is going on. Sometimes she even helps protect us and keep us out of trouble. There is a hook in Travel Fish's cockpit where she hangs in between trips.

One time after we returned from a Travel Fish trip, Voice of Travel Fish asked if she could come along with us rather than be left on her hook. "I would like to collect some data for the topic drive of Travel Fish," she said. "I may need some help from you, but I shouldn't be much trouble."

Ginny answered, "It's no trouble at all. You've helped us a lot. It'll be good to help you. You can come home with me tonight."

"Very well," said VTF. "Will you take me with you to school tomorrow?"

"That should be easy enough," Ginny said.

We left the empty lot where we play and headed for home.

The next morning my kid sister Molly and I met Ginny in front of her house, and we walked to the school bus stop together. Ginny pulled VTF out of her backpack and said, "Good morning, Voice! Are you ready to collect your data?"

"Good morning, Ginny. Hello to you, Johnny and Molly! I am ready. I need two things from you. Ginny, as we ride the bus to school, I'd like you to hold me so that I can see out the window as we travel. I also request that each of you observe your community on the way to school. You will be searching for people who need help.

"Please keep a list. When we get home after school I would like you to report to me all of the people you noted who need help. Do you understand?"

"Got it!" said Molly.

"Okay," said Ginny.

We climbed on the noisy bus and gave Ginny the window seat. She placed Voice of Travel Fish on the ledge of the window facing outside. Then VTF's eyes lit up; we'd never seen that before. I guess she was watching for people who need help.

So we started looking, too. It was more difficult than I thought it would be. I didn't see any old ladies who needed help trying to cross the street. I didn't see any buildings on fire with someone shouting out the window for me to help. I looked for someone who had fallen to the ground and needed help getting up. It was no use—I couldn't find any people who needed help.

Molly and Ginny had the same results. Molly said, "I bet we saw 1,000 people on the way to school, and they all looked just fine."

Ginny wondered, "Do you suppose Voice of Travel Fish can see something we can't?"

"Maybe VTF didn't see anything either," I said. "We'll find out when we get home this afternoon."

We found the same thing in the afternoon that we had in the morning. Nothing.

After the bus dropped us off, we went straight to the empty lot where Travel Fish is hidden.

We climbed over the tire pile and into Travel Fish and put VTF on the dashboard. Her eyes finally stopped glowing and she asked us, "Hello, kids. Do you have your lists?"

We explained that we had seen all kinds of people doing all kinds of things, but we didn't see anyone who needed help.

VTF said, "Please watch."

A slot opened on top of the dashboard and a monitor rose up. There's always something new with Travel Fish. The screen came to life and the first thing we saw was a video of our trip to school. VTF must have recorded it with her eyes.

I remembered the stuff we were seeing from earlier that day. The screen showed our post office and paused. VTF spoke up, "There. Do you see the elderly man coming out of the post office?"

We all said that we did.

"He went there to change his mailing information. He had to remove his wife's name from his mailings because she died last month. He has no children or other family."

Molly asked, "Is he all alone?"

"That's right," VTF answered.

"Oh," said Molly in a small voice.

The video continued to show us the bus trip through downtown. It passed the library, the movie theater, and several other stores. It paused again. VTF asked, "What do you notice about this line of stores?"

We concentrated on the storefronts. Ginny saw it first. "The card shop is closed."

"So what?" I asked.

VTF said, "That card shop has been open every

day for 36 years. Today is the first day it has not been opened in the morning. Mrs. Martin is home caring for her grandson. His parents are unable to care for him so he lives with Mrs. Martin now. She can't take care of the store and the child."

We watched as the school bus turned a corner to go through a neighborhood. I remembered the city bus that was now pulling away from a bus stop. The video stopped again.

I beat VTF to the point, "I see the lady and kids who just got off the bus. They don't look like they need help."

"They are the reason I stopped the video," she said. "Describe what you see."

I looked closer at the monitor, "Well, she's carrying three bags of groceries. And she has two small children walking with her."

VTF agreed, "Very good. She has just come from the grocery store. This bus stop is the closest to her apartment, but she still has to walk many blocks home."

"That'll be hard with all those groceries," Molly said.

Ginny added, "It'll be even harder with those kids. She has to keep an eye on them, too."

"Now you are beginning to understand," said Voice of Travel Fish.

The video went like that for the rest of the trip to school as well as the trip home.

When VTF was finished she had shown us 19 people who needed help. Some of them were worse off than others but one thing was clear: People need help.

"Each of you belongs to Jesus," VTF reminded us.

"So do all the people you saw in this video. Do you know what that means?"

"We're lucky?" Molly wondered.

"No," said Ginny, "that's not it. They belong to Jesus. We belong to Jesus. That means we belong with those people who need help."

"Exactly," said Voice of Travel Fish.

"But that's just depressing," I said. "There are too many people, and we're just kids. How can the three of us help each of those people? It seems hopeless."

VTF assured us, "First you must simply know this truth: People need help. They must not be forgotten. Also remember that it is not up to you alone to care for them. It is up to God, and God will use you. All of God's people must care for those in need."

So that was the day Travel Fish taught us to look at the world through God's eyes and to spot people who need help. Ever since then I don't just see people around town; I see people who need the kind of help that Jesus can give.

Ginny Stayput and the Case of the Shrinking Lunch

Why do I serve others?

Because Christians are servants

My friend Ginny Stayput notices things. I notice things, too, like when my kid sister gets the last piece of cake or that the guy in the baseball movie I am watching was in an astronaut movie last year. Ginny notices important stuff about other people, like the time she noticed that Lydia Kipp's lunches were getting smaller.

Lydia is a friend of Li Yang who is a friend of Ginny, so they were both at the table with us. We were all talking about our spelling test and whether or not *its* is spelled *i-t-s* or *i-t-'-s.*

As we were walking out after lunch Ginny whispered to me, "Did you see what Lydia had for lunch?"

Usually if someone says something like that to you it's because they are picking on another kid. Not Ginny. She doesn't pick on people. I said, "No. I barely remember what I had for lunch. How could I notice Lydia's lunch?"

"It looked normal enough," she said. "She had some carrot sticks and half of an apple. But her sandwich was just one piece of bread folded in half. I don't think it even had anything on it except butter. All she had to drink was a bottle of water that was half empty."

"So?" I asked.

"So it doesn't seem like a whole lunch. Stuff was missing," Ginny said.

I didn't know what to say about that, so I didn't say anything.

Guess what? The next day, Lydia had exactly the same thing for lunch.

Ginny started keeping track of Lydia's lunches. On Wednesday she had almost the same thing as the first two days but her one-piece-of-buttered-bread-and-nothing-else sandwich was made with the heel. On Thursday there was no sandwich.

Friday there was just half an apple, some crackers, and the water bottle. By then even I was beginning to notice Lydia's shrinking lunch.

Ginny said, "I think Lydia was trying to hide her lunch today. It was like she didn't want anyone to see what she had. Or what she didn't have."

"Well, maybe she noticed you've been spying on her lunch every day this week and she didn't want you gawkin' at her food," I said.

"Stop it," Ginny complained. "I'm not spying. I'm worried about her. It's like she doesn't have enough to eat. We should do something."

"What can a couple of kids do?" I asked.

"I'm not sure . . . yet," she said.

Over the weekend I forgot about other people's lunches.

Do you remember how we discovered what Travel Fish actually was when we accidentally traveled into the Bible? Well, on the Sunday after Lydia Kipp's lunches started to shrink we had another accidental trip.

We were goofing around in Travel Fish's cockpit. You probably won't be surprised to hear that my sister Molly and I were fighting. She stood up real fast to punch me in the arm, but instead she banged her head on the purple button.

Somehow the dials were set for John 14:12. It was there that we heard Jesus giving a sermon. He said that part of believing in him was doing the things he did. That kinda scared me. I mean, Jesus did some amazing things. But he did some scary things, too. I wasn't sure I could walk on water or talk to demons. I figured it would take me a while to figure out what that means.

On Monday, Lydia was back to a one-piece-of-buttered-bread-and-nothing-else sandwich. This time it was a regular piece of bread and not the heel.

Ginny gobbled up an apple, a cupcake, some carrots, and her juice box. She ate real fast like a monkey who's worried that the other monkeys are going to steal her food. I stared at her the whole time. It was kinda gross to watch, but it was kinda cool, too.

She picked up the last thing in her lunchbox—the sandwich. She said, "Boy, I'm full already, and I haven't even touched my ham sandwich. Does anyone want it?"

I said, "Ooh! Dibs! I'll take it." **WHACK!** Ginny kicked me hard in the shin.

"**YOW!** I mean . . . never mind," I said. "I guess I'm full too."

Ginny turned to Lydia. "How about you Lydia? Have you got room for a sandwich?"

Lydia looked at her like maybe she was waiting for Ginny to pull the sandwich away and start laughing at her.

"I s'pose," she said quietly. "Thanks." She took the sandwich and started to eat it slowly. She held the sandwich close to her chest and stared at the top of the table as she chewed. She finished half of it and carefully wrapped up what was left. "Excuse me." She got up from the table.

The kindergartners had just arrived in the lunchroom. Lydia walked over and stood by her kid sister Brenda. She handed her the second half of the ham sandwich. She looked back at Ginny and me. We turned our eyes back to our lunches right away, but I think Lydia caught us staring at her. She rushed out of the lunchroom. Brenda looked so happy that you would've thought someone had just given her a puppy for Christmas.

"Oh man," I whispered. "Something's wrong there." Ginny looked real sad. I asked her, "You weren't really full, were you?"

She was watching Brenda gobble the sandwich. "No," she said. "But I don't really feel like eating now."

Ginny was real quiet for the rest of the day. She was sad that Lydia and Brenda didn't have real lunches. And she was curious about why their lunches were shrinking. But most of all she was making a plan.

She gave me the plan when we walked home from school. "Tell your dad that you've been hungry after lunch. Ask him to give you some extra stuff. Extra fruit, extra sandwich, extra juice box, anything he'll give you. I'll do the same with my mom. We'll share our extras with Lydia Kipp and her sister."

My dad acted sort of suspicious when I asked for an extra sandwich the next morning. He warned me that I'd better not waste it. I promised not to.

I squirreled away an extra juice box before I left for school. Molly and I met Ginny in front of her house. Right away she asked, "Did you get extra lunch?"

I told her about the extra sandwich and juice.

Molly started complaining, "You got extra lunch? No fair!"

"Stop hollering, Molly," I hollered. "It's not for me."

"What are you gonna do? Give your teacher a sandwich so that you can be teacher's pet?" she teased.

Ginny stepped in. "Do you know Brenda Kipp, Molly?"

"Yeah, she sits two desks ahead of me in class," said Molly.

"Well, her sister Lydia is in our class. We noticed that their lunches have been shrinking."

"How come?" Molly asked.

Ginny thought for a bit. "I'm not sure why. I've been trying to figure it out. Maybe one of their parents lost a job so they can't afford a whole lunch."

Molly had her own harebrained idea, "Maybe their parents got abducted by aliens in a flying saucer and they're living all alone and that's all they know how to make for lunch. Man, if our parents got abducted by aliens I would want cupcakes and chocolate milk in my lunch. No. Wait! I would stop going to school if Mom and Pop got abducted. I'd sit home all day and watch *Fish Whisperer* and *Vets in Practice*. Then I'd . . ."

She went on like that until we got to school. We warned her not to pick on Brenda or ask her any stupid questions. She said her teacher always tells the class that there's no such thing as a stupid question. Then she waltzed into her classroom.

At lunch that day it was just Ginny, Lydia, and me at the table. Ginny and I emptied out our lunch bags.

"Oh brother," I said. "My Dad made me two sandwiches. What a goof!"

Ginny chimed in, "What a coincidence! I have an extra sandwich, too. And two juice boxes."

"Why, I have an extra juice as well," I said. "I'd certainly hate to waste this stuff." I looked at Lydia. I could tell right away that I was a terrible actor and I had blown it.

Lydia asked, "What are you guys doing?"

I froze. My scalp tingled. What could I say?

Good old Ginny. She fessed up and told Lydia that we were worried about her and her sister and their shrinking lunches. She told her about our plan to bring some extra food for them. It was silent at our table for about a thousand minutes. We didn't eat. We didn't drink. My scalp wouldn't stop burning with prickly heat.

I thought Lydia would cry and run away or something.

She finally said, "Thanks." She took the sandwiches and juice boxes. She ate the peanut butter sandwich that my dad had made and drank Ginny's white cranberry juice.

I asked, "How come your lunches have been shrinking?"

She stopped chewing and looked at the table. "Can we not talk about it?"

"Sure," said Ginny.

The kindergarten class came in just as Lydia finished up her lunch. "Thanks. I mean it. Thanks." She stood up and met her kid sister. She gave her the lunch and pointed over at us. Brenda smiled and waved a little wave before she sat down to eat.

Ginny and I didn't speak. We just finished the last bit of our juice and headed back to class.

That night as I lay in bed I remembered what Jesus said about acting like him if we believe in him. Is that what we were doing with our lunches? How did we end up accidentally going to just the right place in the Bible? Maybe there aren't any accidents with Travel Fish.

Hey, Hey, I've Got to Pray

How does God get us ready to serve?

God listens when we pray

I was doing my worst ever Saturday morning chore—taking out the garbage—when I spotted my best ever friend—Ginny Stayput—sitting on her porch and looking sad. Or was she looking mad? I plopped down the last week's chicken bones and empty toothpaste tubes and crossed my yard over to her house.

"Hi, Ginny."

"Hrrump!"

That answered my question. She was MAD. "What are you so angry about?"

"My mom, that's what I'm mad about."

"What about her?" I asked.

"She volunteered me to pray the prayers in the

worship service tomorrow. She didn't ask me, she just told me. I told her I don't want to do it. She said my name's already printed in the bulletin so there's nothing we can do about it!"

You may or may not know this but Ginny's mom is the pastor at St. Dysmas, which is our church.

I felt for Ginny. I'd rather eat squid than do anything in worship.

"The problem is I've never prayed in front of all those people before. I can sing in front of them. I can read the Bible lesson in front of that many people. But I don't know about praying out loud. Everyone's going to expect me to pray like my mom does. Just because I'm the pastor's kid doesn't mean I can do everything a pastor can do."

"Well, good thing for you we've got a friend like Travel Fish," I said.

"What?" she challenged me. "You want Travel Fish to pray instead of me?"

"No. But don't you suppose people prayed in the Bible?"

She slapped her forehead. "Of course! Maybe Travel Fish can take us to some prayers in the Bible."

We got my kid sister Molly and then we all raced to the empty lot and climbed up the pile of tires. Inside the pile is the secret place where we found Travel Fish.

Travel Fish opened its door for us. Once we got inside Ginny picked Voice of Travel Fish off her hook. The peaceful Voice greeted us. "Hello, kids. Where are we going today?" VTF asked.

"Can you help us figure out where to go, VTF?" asked Molly.

"Certainly. How may I be of assistance?" VTF answered.

I asked, "Where in the Bible can we learn something about praying?"

VTF said, "Prayers are prevalent throughout the Scriptures. Whenever people speak to God or listen to God they are praying. It will not be difficult to find prayer in the Bible. It will be difficult to narrow down your choices."

Ginny asked, "Where's the best place to go?"

"You will need more than one passage. Perhaps today is the day for you to discover the Theme Drive of Travel Fish."

"What's the Theme Drive?" I asked.

VTF answered, "So far you have only traveled to specific passages by setting the dashboard dials and buttons to the book, chapter, and verse. The Theme Drive will rapidly take you to several passages that relate to the theme you choose. In this case you will witness several confession prayers." We heard a click as a door on the dashboard slid open. It revealed a small keyboard and screen. "I invite you to enter a topic into the Theme Drive."

Ginny leaned forward and typed the word *pray*.

VTF continued, "Now you may push the purple button." I reached to tap the button that would bring us into the Bible.

The next morning, my family and I were sitting in our favorite spot in church. I waved at Ginny. She didn't look nervous at all. When the time came for her to pray Ginny got up and walked toward the altar. As she stood next to it, she stopped and took off her shoes.* I can't say I've ever seen Pastor Stayput do this for the prayers.

All around us people started *whispering* and giggling. But it didn't phase Ginny. She left her shoes and walked behind the altar. The congregation got quiet again as Ginny raised her hands.✓ This was something folks were used to. That's how Pastor Stayput does it. But then Ginny started praying.

What came out of her mouth was a mixture of hollering and singing. "Holy, holy, holy is the Lord of hosts; the whole earth is full of his glory," she prayed.*

Usually people sort of look down or close their eyes during the prayers at church. I watched as people stopped looking at the tops of their shoes and sort of peeked up at Ginny. They were probably glad they did look up at her, too, because the way Ginny was doing it you had to see her pray just as much as you had to hear her pray.

She swung her arms down and ran around to the front of the altar. She fell down to her knees and kept her arms high in the air.▲ She kept praying in that loud, sing-songy hollering voice. "Dear God, you know everything about me and everything about all of us.◆ You know what? That scares me because it means you know the mean stuff I think about Donnie Brook and other bullies. It means you know all the rotten stuff I do that I wish was a secret."

Boy, she was on a roll!

Next, she laid herself down, face first, flat on the floor. People weren't just peeking at her now; they were staring at her with bug-eyes.❖

"Oh God! Please forgive us for our sins. You could treat us mean because we are mean. But please treat us nice because you are nice."✖

Then she stood up again and stared straight up at the ceiling, "You promised, God. You promised to love us and forgive us. You don't want people to think you're a joker do you? You don't want people to think that you promise to love us but then are mean to us, do you?"*

People stood staring at her with their mouths open. It was quieter than a candlelight service in there.

My kid sister Molly said, "Cool!" And she didn't whisper it.

"SHUSH!" my dad scolded. He wasn't whispering either.

An "Amen!" came from the other side of the church. It was Ginny's mom, Pastor Stayput. Ginny picked up her shoes and walked back to the front row. Her mom came to the front and told everyone that God does forgive us. Piano music started, and we all started singing the next song.

Church kind of got back to normal after that. Once worship was finished I walked over to Ginny and said, "Well . . . your mom probably wasn't expecting *that*."

Just then her mom came over to us. Ginny asked, "Am I in trouble, Mom?"

"Trouble? Why would you be in trouble? Those were very biblical prayers. You really did your homework, didn't you?"

Ginny answered, "I was really scared, Mom. I don't know how to pray in front of people. So I got some help to look in the Bible to figure out how to pray."

Pastor Stayput asked, "Who helped you?"

"Travel . . . um, I mean, Johnny did."

"Well, you two found some great prayers and postures in the Bible. It has lots of wonderful examples of prayer. But sweetie, there's something much more important than posture or fancy vocabulary words for praying."

Molly asked, "What?"

"Think about it," she said. "With all the different sorts of prayers in the Bible, what is the one thing they have in common?"

We couldn't think of anything.

Ginny's mom asked, "When the Egyptians were chasing Moses and his people, and the Red Sea was in front of them, Moses asked God for help. What happened?"

"I know!" I said. "God spread open the sea and the people got away."

"Exactly," she said. "And what happened when Moses told God the people of Israel were hungry and needed food?"

Ginny answered this one. "God gave them manna to eat."

"Right. No matter whether they stood or lay down; no matter what they did with their hands or what sort of words they used, what is the one thing all the prayers in the Bible and all our prayers have in common?"

"God hears them all," we both answered.

"Good," her mom said. "We pray to God because we know God hears us and wants to take good care of us."

Ginny said, "Okay. I've learned a lot about praying, but is it okay if I don't have to do it at worship again for a while?"

"Definitely."

Here are the places in the Bible that inspired Ginny's prayers and postures:

- Exodus 3:4-6
- 1 Timothy 2:8
- Isaiah 6:2-4
- Luke 22:41
- Psalm 139
- Matthew 26:39
- Psalm 51
- Exodus 17:2-4

Donkey See, Donkey Do

How does God get us ready to serve?

God speaks to us

My nose hairs and my earlobes were all tingly, and I smelled the smell of sour apple gummy worms.

My kid sister Molly hooted, "That was awesome!"

"Who would have thought that being chased by an entire army would be so cool?" I said.

"It helped that we knew the end of the story," said my best friend Ginny. "Otherwise we would have been scared stiff."

Travel Fish had returned us from Exodus 14 where God split the Red Sea open and the people of Israel zipped across it to escape the Egyptian army. Even though Israel got away clean it was the Egyptians who took a bath.

Travel Fish opened its door, and Stripe jumped out. Ginny

and Molly climbed out. I climbed out. And then a donkey climbed out.

Molly yelled, "Wow! A donkey!"

"A donkey? How did a donkey get in here?" I asked. "What are we going to do with a donkey?"

"We can keep it in my room," said Molly. "I'll feed him and wash him and play with him and I'll call him George."

"We can't keep a donkey! We already have a pet," I said. Stripe barked in agreement. "Besides, the donkey stinks."

"You're no bed of roses yourself, kid," the donkey replied.

We all screamed, "YAAAAA!"

"Listen," he said, "I'm pretty hungry. Where can a beast of burden get a little lunch? You got any oats or grass or something?"

Ginny ran back inside and grabbed Voice of Travel Fish. She said, "Voice, we seem to have come home with an extra passenger!"

"Please explain," VTF said.

"A donkey came back with us," Ginny explained. "And it's talking!"

VTF said, "You must be speaking of Balaam's donkey."

"Who's Balaam?" I asked.

The donkey spoke up, "Balaam is my master."

Ginny asked VTF, "But how did he get back here with us?"

"It *is* quite odd," VTF said. "There must be a glitch in Travel Fish's programming. I will need to go into a search mode. Ginny, please place me on the dashboard of Travel Fish so I can communicate with its system. For a brief time I will be out of communication with you. May I suggest that while you wait you ask the donkey to explain ways in which God communicates with people?"

Ginny put VTF back in Travel Fish. I said, "How about it, donkey? Do you know anything about how God talks to people?"

"I've got an idea or two," he said. "But first I want to show you how to get a donkey to talk."

"But you're already talking," Molly said.

"Well, I ain't saying another word until I've got something yummy in my tummy." He sat down and stared at us like a spoiled kid who wants a new toy.

"Well, what in the world does a donkey eat? Tin cans or something?" I asked.

"You're thinking of goats," Ginny said.

Molly said, "He asked if we have grass. Let's take him to our yard!"

"I don't know if that's such a good idea, Molly. What if someone sees us? How are we going to explain why we have a donkey?"

"We'll just say I got it for my birthday," she answered.

Ginny finally spoke up, "No, Molly, I agree with Johnny. It's too risky to walk down the street with a donkey. Let's take him over to the river. There's some tall grass over there, and we won't have to go past any houses."

"Sound okay to you, donkey?" I asked.

He stuck his nose in the air and looked away like I had offended him. "Harrumph."

"C'mon, Mr. Donkey!" Molly whined. "The grass is really green over by the river. That's all we have."

He let out a big sigh. "Oh, all right. Let's go."

We took him to the river and watched him eat. He kept his word and didn't say a thing to us until his tummy was full. Once he was done munching he said, "That hit the spot. Now, what was I supposed to tell you about?"

"You were going to tell us ways that God speaks to people," Molly said.

"Well, you're looking at one of the ways right now," he said.

All three of us looked around to see who or what he was talking about. None of us saw anything that looked like God speaking to us.

"No," said the donkey. "Look at me. *Then* you're looking at one of the ways God has spoken."

"You're crazy," Molly said.

"I'm crazy?" he asked. "You kids are sitting by a river talking to a donkey, and you say *I'm* crazy?"

"Good point," Ginny said. "So tell us your story."

"Don't mind if I do. You see, I had been Balaam's donkey ever since he was knee high to a grasshopper. I took him wherever he wanted to go. He fed me crunchy oats and sweet, sweet grass. Mmm, Mmm! It was a lot better than these weeds you fed me.

"Balaam was a prophet of God. That's one of the ways God talks to people, too—through prophets. They're like messengers for God."

The donkey told us how some of Israel's enemies wanted Balaam to help them win a battle. They knew he had God's power and they wanted him to be on their side.

Balaam was riding his donkey to go help them with the battle but an angel of God stood in the path. The donkey saw the angel and couldn't go around it.

"So I did what came naturally," the donkey said. "I lay down right there. But you see, Balaam couldn't see the angel. He thought I was just being lazy so he smacked my behind. Three times!"

"That was too much. So I opened my mouth but it wasn't a 'Hee' that came out or a 'Haw.' It was real words. I was just as surprised as he was. I told him about the angel in our way. And you know what? As soon as I said that . . . POW! Balaam could see the angel, too.

"Angels are another way God has spoken to people. That's how God spoke to Balaam. The angel told him that he'd better not help the enemies . . . or else."

"Or else what?" Ginny asked.

"Or else he'd be in big trouble. That's what else," said the donkey. "That angel wasn't carrying a harp. It was carrying a sword as long as my leg."

Molly chimed in, "Then it's a good thing you laid down."

"You've got that right," said the donkey. "I'm a life-saving donkey now. He's been treating me real good ever since then. Now as far as I know, I am the only talking donkey in the world. But that God of ours never stops talking. I'm living proof that God will do whatever it takes to get the message across to you. Sometimes it's real obvious. Sometimes God's not so obvious about it."

The donkey must have really loved to talk because he wouldn't stop. He told us a bunch of ways God has spoken. Sometimes God skipped angels and donkeys and God's voice just came out of nowhere to talk to people. God has kids talk for him sometimes. There are places in the Bible when God spoke to people in dreams. One time some writing appeared on a wall at a party.

"I've never had dreams like that," I complained. "And the only time I've seen writing on the wall was when Molly used a marker to write her name on the kitchen wall."

"Yeah," Molly said, "I got in big trouble for that. Did God get in trouble for writing on the wall?"

"Nope. When you're God you get to do stuff like that," said the donkey.

"Why doesn't God talk to us anymore?" asked Ginny.

"Are you kidding? God hasn't stopped talking! I'll let you in on a secret. There's no problem with the Travel Fish thingy. And I didn't end up here by accident. You are having a conversation with a donkey, child. Do you *really* think God doesn't talk to you today?"

With that the donkey got up. "It's time for me to go back now. I'm supposed to tell you kids to talk to each other and figure out ways that God does speak to you today. And God *does* speak to you nowadays. Am I right, Stripe?"

"Woof!" said Stripe, which I suppose meant, "Yes."

We all walked back to Travel Fish and the donkey climbed in. "So long," he said, "and thanks for the grass." The door shut and we turned to walk home.

Molly looked as Stripe as we walked and said, "You tell us if there's any angels in our way, okay, Stripe?"

"Okay," he said.

490

How does God get us ready to serve?

God forgives us

Travel Fish took us to Matthew 18 where we heard Jesus say that when it comes to forgiving, once just isn't enough. He can't get enough of it; and since we are forgiven, we should forgive others. Voice of Travel Fish suggested that we make a list of times we've read about God's forgiveness in the Bible. Then VTF said we should each make a list of the times we had forgiven someone else. Here's what I have so far:

Here's a list of sins that people in the Bible confessed to God	Here's a list of sins that God forgives
• Worshiping a statue of a cow	• Worshiping a statue of a cow
• Killing	• Killing
• Stealing	• Stealing
• Cheating	• Cheating
• Just being plain ol' nasty	• Just being plain ol' nasty

Times I've needed forgiveness

- Calling my sister Molly a rat fart
- Forgetting to feed my dog Stripe (a bunch of times)

- Forgetting to tell my dad that his boss called

- Hating Donnie Brook and wishing bad things would happen to him
- Taking some Halloween candy from my sister's stash

- Being jealous when we got the newest, coolest Big Jim action figure as a Christmas gift for a needy family (I wanted to keep it for myself so I pitched a fit)
- Cheating
- Just being plain ol' nasty

That's as far as I've gotten right now.

Here's a list of times I've forgiven other people.

- When my sister Molly called me a rat fart
- Donnie Brook for doing mean stuff to me

- My dad for hollering at me about the busted screen in the patio door (even though I told him a bunch of times that I didn't do it)
- Molly for not confessing it was her who busted the screen in the patio door (even when she knew Dad was hollering at me about it)
- My sister for taking candy out of my Christmas stocking

There's probably more than that but this is as far as I got right now.

I know there are a bunch more sins. I'm just starting to learn this stuff though.

Believe It!

How does God get us ready to serve?

God helps us believe in Jesus

Many of the times when Travel Fish took us back to see the disciples they were whispering and hiding out because they were scared that the people who killed Jesus on the cross might do the same to them.

The scariest time was just after the first Easter. We traveled back to see what it was like when Jesus visited them after he walked out of his grave. Travel Fish took us to John 20:26. We were in a dark little room. The doors and windows were shut tight. Even though I knew Jesus was alive, I thought it felt kind of eerie in there.

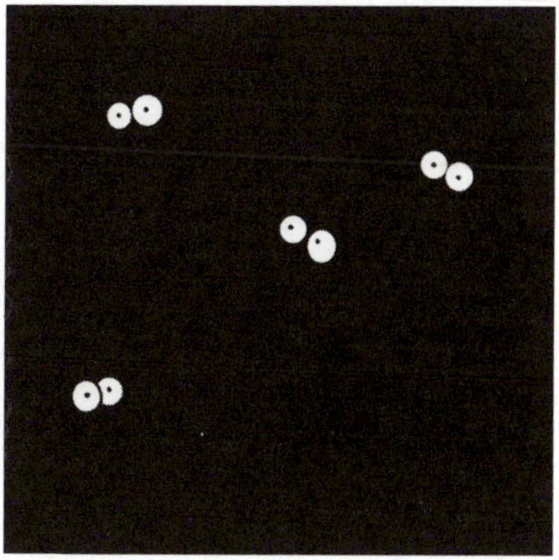

Our new old friend Bart—his name is really

Bartholomew and he's a disciple—told us that most of the disciples had already seen Jesus alive again. Thomas was the only one who hadn't.

The last time Thomas had seen him was when Jesus was dying. Thomas was treating the other disciples like they were silly for believing that Jesus was alive again. He was talking all smart, "Unless I see the mark of the nails in his hands and place my finger into the mark of the nails and place my hand into his side, I will *never* believe."

The other disciples were trying to convince Thomas that they really had seen Jesus. But he just wouldn't believe it. He repeated what he had said about touching the hole in Jesus' side and then—WHAM—there was Jesus.

Jesus didn't holler at Thomas though, even though Thomas was being sort of bullheaded about the resurrection. Thomas stood there with his mouth wide open. I think he was trying to decide if he was looking at a ghost.

"Peace be with you," Jesus said. Then he held out his hands and said to Thomas, "Put your finger here, and see my hands; and put out your hand, and place it in my side. Do not disbelieve, but believe."

When Thomas could finally spit out words, the first thing he said was, "My Lord and my God!"

This is when Jesus did scold him a little. "Have you believed because you have seen me? Blessed are those who have not seen and yet have believed." But even then, he wasn't being too rough on Thomas.

We hung out for a while and watched the reunion. The disciples even shared some fish with us. I could

have used a little tartar sauce with mine but it hadn't been invented yet. Jesus taught the disciples some important last-minute stuff, like that they would be able to forgive people and it would be just like Jesus was forgiving them.

Jesus patted Stripe on the head and gave him a bit of fish. Stripe doesn't get table scraps at our house. I think Jesus was kind of spoiling my dog. But what are you going to do if the Son of God is spoiling your dog—tell him to quit?

Jesus told us that when people couldn't see *him*, they would see *us*. We would be the ones who share him with other people.

After a while we said goodbye to all the others. They all looked up and waved goodbye, except Thomas. He couldn't take his eyes off of Jesus.

We climbed in to Travel Fish and pushed the button for home.

My nose hairs and my earlobes were all tingly, and I smelled the smell of sour apple gummy worms. We said goodbye to Voice of Travel Fish.

As we climbed out of the old pile of tires I said to Ginny, "I can't remember a time when I didn't believe in Jesus. Can you?"

"No," she answered. "For as long as I can remember Mom and Dad have always been telling me about how I am baptized and I belong to Jesus."

"You know what that means, don't you?" I asked Molly. "It means we're blessed. Jesus said so."

"That's right. We believed in Jesus before Travel Fish brought us back to see him," Ginny added.

I pointed out that there are lots of folks who don't believe in Jesus.

"Are they all named Thomas?" Molly wanted to know.

I said, "No, you goof. There are way too many people who don't believe in Jesus to have them all be named Thomas."

"Ginny?" she asked, "Are there really a lot of people who don't believe in Jesus?"

"Sure," she answered. "There are some people who haven't even *heard* of him."

Molly pondered that as we walked, which means she thought real hard about it. Finally she got real serious and said, "Then we're going to have to tell them."

I've got to tell you that this made me sort of *nervous*.

I know it's impossible for three kids to tell every person on the entire planet about Jesus. But even if we could, how do we make them believe?

We got to Ginny's house. She ran inside and got us some ice pops: green for me, red for Molly, and orange for herself. We sat on the front steps and started eating them. Stripe sat close to Molly because she is the most likely to drop food. He was ready to swoop in like a vacuum cleaner if she did. A drool bomb was hanging off his mouth.

I asked, "Even if we only had to tell *one* person, how would we get them to believe in Jesus if they didn't want too? What are we going to do, hold them in a headlock until they believe?"

"I'll do that!" cheered Molly.

"Oh sure," I sneered, "you barely know how to tie your shoes. How could you know something like this?"

She wasn't phased by my mean question. She fed some of her ice pop to Stripe. Then she said, "I *do* know how to tie my shoes and I *do* know something about helping God plant stuff."

Even Ginny had to ask, "What are you talking about?"

Molly kept right on going. "'Remember one of our trips in Travel Fish when we saw God planting flowers?"

"Yeah," I said. "That was the second creation story."

Ginny jumped in, "Oh yeah! You helped God plant flowers."

"So did Stripe," added Molly.

"Woof," woofed Stripe.

"I planted some of those flowers. But did I make them grow? *No*. I put one in the dirt and went to the next one. There were red ones, yellow ones, green ones, purple ones, and blue ones. But no matter what color I planted or how much dirt I put on them I couldn't make them grow."

"Only God could do that," I finished for her. I had to admit it. Not only did my kid sister *understand*, she helped me to understand.

"God helps us believe in Jesus. With the Bible, with people who love us, with our baptism, with the Holy Spirit, God helps us believe." I couldn't quite believe that I'd figured all that out because of what Molly said.

"Well, Johnny Dakota," said Ginny, "is there anything you need to say to your wise little sister?"

I stood up. "Hear ye! Hear ye! For the first and probably the last time, I, Johnny Dakota, have learned something from my kid sister." I sat back down. We finished our ice pops and spent the rest of the day looking at clouds.

Holy Spirit Zip Drive

How does God get us ready to serve?

God fills us with the Holy Spirit

"I'm bored," said my sister Molly.

"Stop saying that," I scolded her. "We could be in the house watching *Attack of the Space Fleas* if you wouldn't have been such a jerk."

"I hate the *Space Fleas*. It's too scary! I want to watch *The Mangles*," she whined.

"They are so goofy. Their songs are stupid rip-offs of real songs. That's a baby show."

In case you haven't guessed yet, Molly and I had been arguing about what to watch on TV. We fight about that a lot. Well, our parents had enough so they booted us outside and told us that there would be no TV for the rest of the weekend. We were supposed to enjoy the great outdoors or something.

Now we were both bored.

"Hey, you two!" It was our neighbor and my best friend Ginny Stayput. She sat on the steps with us.

"Hi, Ginny. Johnny got us in trouble and now our parents might not ever let us back in the house."

I said, "*I* didn't get us in trouble, *you* got us in trouble!"

"Surprise, surprise. The Dakota kids are fighting. Who would have thought it?" Ginny teased. She sees us fighting a lot. "Why don't you give it a break and go visit Travel Fish with me?"

Molly and I looked at each other, shrugged our shoulders and agreed, "Okay."

Molly said, "That Ginny, she's a miracle worker."

"Yep," Ginny agreed, "getting you two to stop crabbin' at each other is a gift I have."

When we got to Travel Fish and took Voice of Travel Fish off of her hook, I asked, "So, VTF, do you and Travel Fish have anything new for us?"

"As a matter of fact, we do," said VTF. Travel Fish and I have developed a zip drive program. I believe I'll call it the **Holy Spirit Zip Drive.** With it, Travel Fish will be able to quickly and efficiently take you throughout the Bible, stopping briefly at events at which the Holy Spirit had significant impact."

"Cool! Let's go," exclaimed Molly.

"Very well. Please be seated," said VTF.

We took our seats and listened as VTF explained that we would not be getting out of Travel Fish like we usually do. We wouldn't have to set any dials, either. Instead she would get us going by beginning the program that she and Travel Fish had created.

A panel on one of Travel Fish's walls slid open. It was a window and we were looking at the secret place in the pile of tires where Travel Fish is hidden.

VTF said, "Travel Fish, please initiate the **Holy Spirit Zip Drive."**

ZZZZiiiipahhhh

The window flashed a blinding bright green and our heads slammed back in our seats like we were in a rocket ship.

Then the window went black. In the distance we saw bright, colorful clouds of gases. They got bigger and bigger, and we rocketed toward them. Suddenly the black space began to get splattered with white spots.

"Those are planets and stars being created!" Ginny said.

"You are correct," VTF assured her. "Now watch closely."

We shot into one of the clouds and realized we were headed for the earth. We swept down to the surface. It was all water with something like a cloud swirling over the top of it.

"It's beautiful," whispered Molly.

VTF spoke, "You are seeing creation, children. Listen to the word of the Lord. 'And the earth was without form, and void; and darkness was upon the face of the deep. And the Spirit of God moved upon the face of the waters.' This is Genesis chapter 1, verse 2."

The window flashed green again and we saw green land appear.

We saw jungles and grasslands.

We saw dolphins jumping and flipping out of the water.

We saw giraffes and duck-billed platypuses.

The window glowed lime green as VTF said, "The Holy Spirit was present and active at creation. The Holy Spirit was active in thinking of and working toward all things."

"What about after everything was made?" I asked.

"Let's see," VTF said.

The window flashed green again and we were in the desert. Far in the distance we saw a tent. Travel Fish was rocketing toward it. I braced myself because it seemed like we would crash right into it.

We slowed down just in time. Four men were sitting outside the tent. One guy was really old and looked like he'd lived in the desert his whole life. The other three sat close to each other. They sort of glowed.

"Hey, look!" Molly said. She was pointing to the tent. An old lady was peeking out at the men. She started laughing and slapping her knee. She finally laughed so hard that she fell over on her side.

Ginny said, "Oh! That's Abraham and Sarah. They're really old; even older than our grandparents but they never had any kids. Those three guys are the Lord and two angels, and they just told Abraham that the Holy Spirit is going to see to it that they will have a baby soon. Sarah's laughing because she thinks she is too old to have a baby."

Again and again the window flashed bright green showing us person after person who the Holy Spirit helped.

We saw King David confessing his sins and becoming a great king.

We saw Samson, the strongest man in the world.

We saw Solomon, the wisest king Israel ever had.

We saw Mary hearing that she was going to be the mother of God's son.

We saw Mary again having the guts to agree to do it.

The next green flash was awesome. We ended up under water. "Lookit!" I yelled. "That's Jesus. And those are John the Baptist's hands pushing him under the water."

Jesus started to get up out of the water and Travel Fish followed. Above the water we saw John and the big crowd. The crowd looked up in amazement. What looked like a neon dove, all shiny and glowing, was hovering over Jesus. "That is the Holy Spirit," said VTF.

The green flashes raced us through the New Testament.

We saw Jesus arguing with the devil out in the desert.

We saw the scared disciples dodging flames and getting their hair blown around on Pentecost day.

We saw the disciples telling people about Jesus and we saw the people believe.

We saw the disciples healing people.

The next time the window flashed green it stayed green a little longer and we felt Travel Fish racing ahead. The green vanished and we saw that we were in church.

Molly cooed, "It's a baptism. Look at that cute baby."

"Hey Ginny, that's your mom," I said.

"It is! And that's Uncle John and Aunt Laurie . . . Oh! That baby is me. This is my baptism!"

We saw another church, another pastor, and another baby.

"That's Mom and Dad," Molly said. "But where are we?"

"This must be my baptism," I said. We waited to see me get baptized, but instead Dad leaned his head over the font. The pastor doused his head three times. One for the Father. One for the Son. One for the Holy Spirit.

"That's right," I said, "Dad and I got baptized on the same day."

We saw the same church. Mom, Dad, and a three-year-old me were there. This time it was Ginny's mom, Pastor Stayput, who was holding the baby.

"Man," I said, "what a cranky, gross little baby." Molly socked me in the arm as we watched her head get wet, wetter, wettest.

We saw the hidden space inside the pile of old tires.

"Awww," Molly whined. "I don't want to be done with **Holy Spirit Zip Drive."**

"Wait a second. If we were traveling to see how the Holy Spirit works, why did we leave the Bible and go to our baptisms?" I asked.

VTF explained, "The Bible is God's word. But God's word also exists outside the Bible. And the Holy Spirit has not stopped working. The Spirit is busy, even now."

Ginny asked, "But why our baptisms?"

"Because at your baptism you were given the gift of the Holy Spirit. It is the Spirit who gives you faith. It is the Spirit who helps you pray. It is the Spirit who leads you to care for other people the way Jesus takes care of people."

"Awesome!" Molly exclaimed.

"Consider the ramifications, children," said VTF.

I asked, "Come-what the ramifa-who?"

VTF rephrased, "Think about what this means for you and other disciples. Where did we begin the **Holy Spirit Zip Drive?"**

"Right here in the pile of old tires," I answered.

Ginny said, "No, I think she means where our first stop was. It was at creation."

"Yes," said Voice of Travel Fish. "And at each stop along the way you witnessed the mighty power of the Holy Spirit."

"Wow." I was flabbergasted. "The same power that went into creating the stars and everything on earth was in our baptism."

"The same power is in us NOW," pointed out Ginny.

"Precisely." VTF reminded us that the power to believe, the power to pray, and the power to take care of other people are all from the Holy Spirit in us.

Just about every time we walk home from a Travel Fish adventure we are amazed. This time might have been the most amazing. "Just think," I said, "the same Holy Spirit that made the mountains and oceans is the power that makes us disciples."

"And just think," Molly added, "the same Holy Spirit that made snails and lizards is the same power that made you!" And she ran for home with Stripe chasing after her.

Beware the Church Fridge

How does God get us ready to serve?

God gathers us to share meals

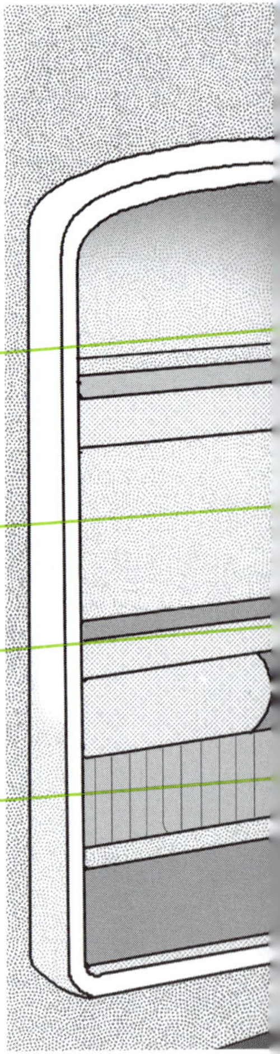

Boiled Easter Eggs: If it is Christmas when you find these, STAY AWAY!

Soda probably won't do any harm, but if the fizz is all gone you will wish you hadn't taken a swig.

If the spaghetti is solid like a rock, you don't want it.

Mystery Item #1: Ask yourself, "What would that be in a fridge?"

Once, after our Sunday school class played a game of Tackle Duck Duck Goose, Ginny and I snuck into the church kitchen to drink milk out of the carton. It wasn't pretty. Here's what I learned. **DON'T JUST TAKE STUFF FROM A CHURCH FRIDGE AND EAT IT!** Here's some stuff to watch out for:

Mystery Item #2: Never eat something you found on top of the church fridge.

Milk should not look like cottage cheese. If the smell burns your nose hairs, DON'T TOUCH!

Pickles can be tricky. They smell the same new as they do old: NASTY!

No food you would ever want to eat would have blue, green, brown, or white fuzz on it. Or pink.

The soda is fresh and new. Do you drink it? Think again. The note behind it says: Property of Pastor Stayput (who happens to be Ginny's mom). Don't touch it!

Lettuce is not supposed to be dark brown. Or liquid. And especially not dark brown liquid.

We eat and have fun at our church, too!

Some of the food we eat at church:

Some people we eat with at St. Dysmas:

My teacher from first grade, Mrs. Zigabreth

Officer Soma (He brought his police car to the church picnic last year!)

Dianna Dexter, the woman who reports the weather on Channel 8

My grandma and grandpa

Mr. Lindgren, my Sunday school teacher

Donnie Brook

Times we eat at our church:

Communion
Easter breakfast
New Member Sunday
Wednesdays in Lent
Wednesdays in Advent
Sick of Winter Picnic
Summer Picnic
After the Sunday school Christmas play (Birthday cake for Jesus!)

When do you eat at your church?

What's your favorite church food?

Who do you sit by when you eat at church?

From the Desk of Mr. Dakota

How does God get us ready to serve?

God teaches us

Hello Readers,

This is Johnny Dakota writing to you, only I'm not a kid anymore. Thanks to Travel Fish, I am able to write you this note from the future—25 years after Ginny, Molly, Stripe, and I first found Travel Fish and VTF.

We are all grown up now. My kid sister Molly isn't a kid anymore. She is married and has three daughters of her own. She is a veterinarian. She and her husband Bart also own a motorcycle shop.

Ginny is a scientist. She, her husband Orlando, and their two sets of twins travel all over the world learning about plants. They are using blueberries to create a tasty medicine that helps forgetful people get better memory. Or was it strawberries to help people with weak ankles get stronger? No, it was blueberries.

I became a teacher for third graders because third graders are some of my favorite people in the whole world. I have a new dog now. He is black and white, but not with spots. His name is George.

Nope, I'm not a kid anymore, but I will never forget Travel Fish and all the adventures it brought us to in the Bible. I know now that it wasn't an accident that we found Travel Fish. God used Travel Fish to teach us.

God taught us with the Bible. God taught us with the people around us. Adults, kids, strangers, and friends all are part of the way God teaches us. God can even use donkeys and Dalmatians to teach us.

God taught me that I am loved even when I'm messy or silly or forgetful or verbose. Verbose means that sometimes I'm long winded—which means that sometimes I talk (or write) more than I need to.

God taught me that Jesus loves all people, even people I do not like very much. (By the way, Donnie Brook is now one of the pastors of St. Dysmas Church. Things changed for him. We are buddies now. But that's a story from our high school years. Maybe I can share it with you another time.)

God used Travel Fish to teach us that when we belong to Jesus we belong to each other, too. And when we are loved by Jesus we get to love other people because Jesus loves them.

One of my favorite things that God has taught me is that all of Christ's people are disciples. Disciples are not just those 12 guys from the Bible. I was a disciple when I was a kid; so were Ginny and Molly. Motorcycle mechanics, school teachers, scientists, veterinarians, grown-ups, and kids all get to be disciples.

God hasn't stopped teaching me either.

I guess my double extra favorite thing that I keep learning is that God came looking for us the way parents look for their kid who is lost in the mall. That's cool. Oh, and that God is always with me. That's cool, too.

Travel Fish is still out there, taking kids on adventures. I wonder who those kids are. Are they any of you? I would really like to know how Travel Fish and Voice of Travel Fish are doing so if it is you, you can write me and tell me your story. Just send it to Johnny Dakota.

Sincerely,
Mr. Jonathan Dakota
(Johnny Dakota)

Seasick Rhinoceroses Are No Fun

Where can I serve God?

In my family

Have you ever had to clean up after a seasick rhinoceros? I have. Believe me, it's not pretty. And as if it wasn't bad enough, the whole time I was cleaning rhino vomit and rhino diarrhea my kid sister was petting a koala bear.

Travel Fish had taken us to Genesis 7:24. My best friend Ginny Stayput thought it would be neat to go on Noah's ark. Who could argue with that? I thought it would be a blast to see all the animals on that floating zoo.

Well, we made it to the ark. Unfortunately Travel Fish planted us on the deck of the ark before the rain was over. And it wasn't just rain. It was a downpour, complete with crashing thunder, jagged LIGHTNING, and howling *wind.* The rain stung our faces when we stepped out of Travel Fish. The ark was tilting side to side. I was scared it might tip over.

One of Noah's sons was right there when we stepped out of Travel Fish. It was like he knew we were coming. He shouted over the storm, "You've arrived just in time! Many of the animals are ill from the storm and all this tossing about. We need your hands!

"My name is Shem. Please follow me." He led us inside the ark to the koala bears. He looked at Molly and said, "These creatures are terribly distressed. Someone needs to comfort them and assure them the Lord will protect them. Can you do that?"

Molly shouted, "Can I ever!" She rushed to pick up one of the koalas and it clung to her like she was its mommy. She petted the bear and said, "It's gonna be okay, little bear. I've been in some scary places before and God took good care of me."

Shem led us to a giant bird cage. Shem told Ginny that a door to the cage had come open in the storm. Several birds had escaped. She was going to have to run around to catch them. She would have to be quick to make sure no more birds got out of the cage when she put the escaped birds back in. Ginny didn't seem to mind.

Shem and I kept walking and climbed down some stairs to the lowest level of the ark. The light was very dim. I gasped and held my breath when the smell hit me. Shem said, "Here you go." He was pointing to a pair of rhinoceroses. Now, I always thought rhinos were grey, but this pair was a weird greenish color. Even though I've never seen one close up, I could tell these rhinos looked sick—really sick. Even though I've never smelled one close up, I could tell these rhinos smelled worse than usual. "They're seasick," he said.

The floor all around them was covered with the result of their seasickness. The floor in front of them was a stinky mess. The floor behind them was a steamy mess. Shem handed me a shovel and two big buckets. "I am so grateful that you're here to help," he said. Then he rushed away like a man on a mission. One of the rhinos moaned and gagged. There was another gallon to fill my buckets.

Shem was gone before I could complain, so I got to work. I filled the buckets and started climbing up the stairs. I was on my way out to the deck to dump the bucket over the side. On my way I heard Molly giggling.

"Hey! That tickles," she laughed. She was lying on the floor. The koalas were climbing over her. One was tickling her earlobe. Apparently she was doing a good job of comforting them.

The ark made a huge tilt to the left. One of the buckets sloshed over and spilled on my arm and shirt. Molly saw it happen and looked at me with disgust. "Eww! Get that stuff out of here, Johnny! It's gonna bother the koala bears."

I frowned at her and climbed outside into the storm. By the time I got the buckets dumped over the edge the rainstorm had soaked me to the bone, but at least it washed the rhino vomit off me.

That's how it went the rest of the afternoon—me up and down the stairs with buckets of rhino goo, and my spoiled sister making cute little koala bears think they were on a picnic. I got madder and madder each time I went past them.

I trudged past Molly and her playmates for the tenth time. The koalas were sitting in a little circle with her. She asked them, "Do you know how to play Duck, Duck, Goose?"

That was enough! I blew up. "Geez Louise, Molly! Of course they can't play Duck, Duck, Goose. They're bears! Do you think they went to koala bear vacation Bible school to learn how?"

Molly hollered back, "Stop it, Johnny! You're bothering the koala bears!"

"I don't care about your stupid koala bears! This is just like home. I have to do the nasty stuff, and you get to go on a koala bear picnic!"

Molly had tears in her eyes, but she didn't back down. She never backs down. "Why don't you just go pick up rhino poop, you big rhino butt!"

I yelled, "You're stupid!" I spun around to race back down to the dungeon of seasickness. I didn't get far. Instead I crashed into a skinny old man.

I was relieved when he laughed. "Good thing the buckets were empty, or I'd be covered with you-know-what," he said.

"I'm sorry, sir," I said.

"Please call me Noah," he said. "Shem didn't give you the most glamorous job did he, Johnny?"

"How do you know my name?" I asked.

"The same way I knew to build this big boat," he answered.

I wanted to ask him how that was but I was interrupted by the sound of my sister hollering, "Stop it, mister! I was *supposed* to be playing with them!" I turned around to see a koala bear tug-of-war. A man was trying to pull a koala bear out of Molly's hands. She was holding tight. The bears didn't look so relaxed anymore.

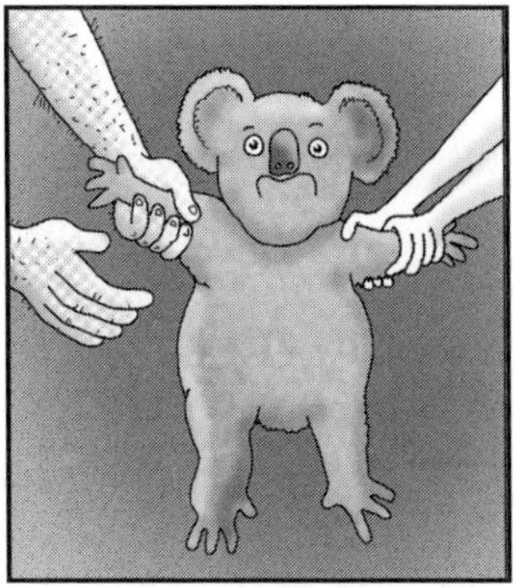

I bolted over to them and jumped on the guy's back. "Leave my sister alone!"

He let go of the bear and spun around. I stuck to his back like bubble gum in long hair. The big oaf tried swatting at me, but couldn't get me.

Noah shouted, "Ham! Stop it now! That child is doing what Shem asked her to do."

The big lug stopped spinning and swatting his back. He looked at Noah. I slid off his back. "Why didn't I know about this? Why is Shem always in charge? You always give him more responsibility than me!"

"Nonsense," replied Noah. "You were busy when we got word that the children would be arriving. Shem was with me, and I sent him to receive them."

"Baah!" growled Ham as he stormed away.

I wanted to know how Noah knew we were coming, but I was more concerned about my kid sister. I turned to her. "Are you okay, Molly?"

She was holding the koala tight, crying softly into its fur. The bear seemed to be petting Molly. "I'm all right," she whispered. I hugged her. It's crazy how I could want to throw her overboard one minute and then want to protect her the next.

Noah put his hand on her shoulder. "I apologize for my son. Sometimes his anger at his brother is more important to him than anything else." He stood back and looked at us. "Don't think for a moment that you are the first or only siblings to fight and love each other at the same time."

"I suppose I did the same thing with my sisters so many years ago. Your children will do the same someday. But remember this. You are gifts from God to each other and to your parents. You are each unique. You are each similar. You are each a blessing. Molly was given the job with the bears because she is gentle and playful. Ginny was put in charge of the birds because she is quick and nimble. Johnny, you had the strength and fortitude for your unpleasant job."

He stopped talking and looked upward. "Ahh. Do you hear that?"

I listened closely. "I don't hear anything."

"Precisely," he said. "The storm is over. Thank you so much for your work. I must go now, and I believe it is time for you to go as well." He patted our heads and walked off.

And just like that, Ginny Stayput walked up to us. Voice of Travel Fish was in her hand. "That was a blast! I was all over this place catching birds. VTF said now that the storm is over we should be going. Hey, how did it go for you guys?"

I answered, "I don't think I ever want to see another rhinoceros."

Molly hugged the koalas and kissed them goodbye.

Travel Fish was waiting on the deck. The sun was shining bright off its side. We climbed in. The door closed, and as Molly reached for the button that would take us home, Ginny crinkled her nose and looked at me. "What's that smell?"

My nose hairs and my earlobes were all tingly, and I smelled the smell of sour apple gummy worms. The juicy robot belch was fading. We were home on the dry land on our tire pile in the empty lot.

Chippy's Cheese Hut—Where a Kid Can Be Wild

Here's a picture of me and my friends at my birthday party.

Where can I serve God?

With my friends

Look on the next two pages to see who everyone is in the picture.

1. Ginny Stayput—Ginny is my double extra best friend and next door neighbor. If any kid is ever alone at lunch or recess, she will hang out with them. We've had a ton of adventures with Travel Fish along with my kid sister Molly and my dalmatian Stripe.

2. Preston Kaiser—Preston lives with his grandparents. He can ride a unicycle. He could write cursive in kindergarten. He plays the piano but never wants anyone to know it.

3. Johnny Dakota—That's me and this is my ninth birthday party at Chippy's Cheese Hut. We played video games, goofed off on the slides and tubes, and ate nine pizzas.

4. Melvin Noy—Melvin is Sheena's twin brother. He can burp the alphabet up to the letter "Q". He loves to tell jokes and will make you laugh if you are having a bad day. Sometimes he leaves our classroom to get special help for reading. He is very allergic to peanut butter.

5. Sheena Noy— She can hop on a pogo stick 203 times without stopping. She has asthma. She isn't afraid of spiders and she's about 15 minutes older than her twin brother Melvin. Oh, she also can wiggle her ears.

6. Kirby Keeble—Kirby has the world's coolest tree house in his backyard. He is deaf and teaches us sign language. My favorite sign is "Silly Turkey." He also taught a bunch of us to sign, "The body of Christ, given for you," and "The blood of Christ, given for you," when we had first communion classes together.

7. Hope Manning—She is shy but she will stand up for any kid that other kids pick on or leave out. She can count to 16 in Chinese and she has a mini-bike. (I kind

of like her, but if you tell anybody I will never tell you another secret again.)

8. Tony Gleed—He's new in our neighborhood so my mom told me to invite him to my party. He is nice. I found out he likes Big Jim action figures as much as I do. Plus he can blow a whole mouthful of milk out his nose. He's obsessed with cars and gave me a model of a 1968 Corvette for my gift.

9. Peter Gooch—His parents own Lolita's Pizza Palace. His birthday party was there last year. He invited our whole class, and we all could make our own pizzas. Peter made a pepperoni pizza with extra licorice toppings. He has a pet parrot that he taught to say, "Polly wants some liver."

10. Lydia Kipp—Lydia started out as just Li's friend. Her dad got hurt and couldn't work. Ginny and I shared our lunches with her for a while. We are pretty good buds now. She gave me a homemade picture frame with a picture of her and Ginny and Li and me.

11. Lars Wynja— He can play guitar and is going to give me lessons for my birthday. He has puked at school at least once a year, every year, since preschool.

12. Li Yang—Likes reading and drawing. She wants to be an illustrator for books someday. She got to go scuba diving in the Bahamas for her vacation last year. She is the most popular girl in our class.

Johnny, Please

Where can I serve God?

At my church

Date/Time: August 24 / 10:05:26 A.M.
10 minutes before worship
Request: "Johnny, would you please run back to my office and get my portable microphone?"
Requested by: Pastor Stayput
Status: Complete
Comments: *It was under her coat and last week's bulletin.*

Date/Time: August 24 / 10:09:19 A.M.
6 minutes before worship
Request: "Young man, could you tell me where the restroom is?"
Requested by: Grandfather of a baby being baptized
Status: Complete
Comments: *He asked me this as I was delivering the microphone to Pastor Stayput.*

Date/Time: September 4 / 11:30:31 A.M.
16 minutes after worship

Request: "Johnny, please hold this umbrella for Mrs. Powell while she waits for her husband to pull the car up to get her."

Requested by: Mrs. Taft, the church secretary

Status: Complete

Comments: *Mrs. Powell is nice. She told me I remind her of her great grandson in Tupelo, Mississippi.*

Date/Time: September 18 / 10:11:03 A.M.
4 minutes before worship

Request: "Say, Johnny, would you help hand out bulletins?"

Requested by: Mr. Lund

Status: Complete

Comments: *I got to help collect the offering, too.*

Date/Time: October 2 | 10:02:55 A.M.
13 minutes before worship
Request: "Sure, Johnny, you can help Ginny take care of the kids in the nursery."
Requested by: Me
Status: Complete
Comments: *I asked Ginny's grandma if I could help them.*

Date/Time: October 2 | 10:45:09 A.M.
during worship
Request: "Oh goodness! The diaper pail in the nursery is full. Johnny would you be a dear and empty it out?"
Requested by: Ginny's grandma
Status: Complete
Comments: *This is the reason I will never ask to help in the nursery again.*

Date/Time: October 23 | 10:52:51 A.M.
near the end of worship
Request: "When you pray this week, please pray for Margaret."
Requested by: Pastor Stayput asked the congregation
Status: Complete
Comments: *I prayed for her every night that week at bedtime.*

Date/Time: October 30 / 10:01:26 A.M.
14 minutes before worship
Request: "Ginny and Johnny, I'd like you to meet Kyle; he is new to St. Dysmas. Would you please show him around and keep him company?"
Requested by: Mr. Albertson (our teacher at school)
Status: Complete
Comments: *It was fun to meet Kyle. He has two dogs.*

Date/Time: November 12 / 10:15:00 A.M.
24 hours before worship
Request: "Johnny, would you please read the Bible verses at worship tomorrow morning?"
Requested by: Pastor Stayput
Status: Complete
Comments: *I read Psalm 50:8–10 and Acts 1:17–19.*

Date/Time: November 27 / 10:10:00 A.M.
5 minutes before worship
Request: "Johnny, would you please light the candles before worship starts?"
Requested by: Mrs. Ramirez
Status: Complete
Comments: *Her son Johnny was supposed to light the candles, but he was sick.*

Date/Time: December 10 / 4:19:01 P.M.
18 hours before worship
Request: "I don't care how that squirrel got in the church; you climb up that Christmas tree and get it out of here!"
Requested by: My dad
Status: Complete
Comments: *It's almost impossible to catch a squirrel if it does not want to be caught.*

Date/Time: December 18 / 6:05:33 P.M.
25 minutes before the Sunday school Christmas pageant
Request: "Johnny! Our Joseph for the Christmas pageant is puking in the restroom! Do you want to clean up after him or act out his part in front of the whole congregation?"
Requested by: Mrs. Gill, the kids' choir director at St. Dysmas
Status: Complete
Comments: *Tough choice. I played Joseph.*

Date/Time: January 15 / 11:30:57 A.M.
15 minutes after worship
Request: "Johnny, I am going to deliver communion to Mr. Gippert today since he couldn't make it to worship today. Would you like to come with me?"
Requested by: My dad
Status: Complete
Comments: *I liked helping this way.*

Date/Time: January 15 / 12:22:06 P.M.
1 hour 7 minutes after worship
Request: "Young man, would you say a prayer, please?"
Requested by: Mr. Gippert
Status: Complete
Comments: *I was surprised but I did it.*

Date/Time: January 27 / 10:08:11 A.M.
6 minutes before worship
Request: "Johnny Dakota, the potato salad from last summer's picnic is trying to escape from the church fridge. Would you clean it up please? And don't eat any of it!"
Requested by: Mr. Stayput, Ginny's dad
Status: Complete
Comments: *I will never eat potato salad again.*

Date/Time: February 12 | 9:05:44 A.M.
5 minutes before Sunday school
Request: "Johnny, be sure to wait outside Molly's classroom after Sunday school gets out. I don't want her to get lost."
Requested by: My mom
Status: Complete
Comments: *Molly crabbed at me for treating her like a little kid.*

Date/Time: March 1 | 7:00:08 P.M.
4 days before worship
Request: "Johnny, I heard that you are taking drum lessons. How would you like to play a drum solo for offering time next Sunday?"
Requested by: Mrs. Gill, the choir director
Status: Complete
Comments: *Mrs. Drummond covered her ears. Her husband was tapping his feet though.*

Date/Time: March 26 | 9:20:32 A.M.
during Sunday school
Request: "Li, would you and Johnny please deliver the Sunday school offering to the office?"
Requested by: Our Sunday school teacher
Status: Complete
Comments: *Easy enough.*

School Lunch Tacos

Where can I serve God?

At my school

I usually eat hot lunch at school except on days when it's going to be something real gross like beef roulade. Do you know what beef roulade is? It's one of the only ways I know that you can ruin beef. It is a slice of roast beef wrapped around a pickle. I'm serious. Look it up on the Internet sometime.

Anyway, the second Tuesday of every month is "Fiesta Day" at the Spelunker Elementary School Gyma-cafeterium. (I gave it that name.) There's nothing better than school lunch tacos. Not everyone agrees with me, but I mean it. Once I even came to school with a fever just because it was the second Tuesday of the month. I didn't care how sick I was—I didn't want to miss school lunch tacos. I'm telling you the truth; after I had one of those school lunch tacos my fever went away and I felt great. It must be something in the grease.

There was a taco day that I wish I could have missed though. It was a few weeks ago. My best friend Ginny

Stayput and I just got our sporks and napkins and we were carrying our trays. I was excited because this particular taco day included Tato Bites with Mexican seasonings on them. Ginny doesn't like Tato Bites so I always get her portion.

I was drooling over my tray trying to decide what I would eat first when Ginny asked the question she asks every day at lunch: "Where do you want to sit?" I looked up from my tray and scanned the gymacafeterium.

There was a table with some of my other friends: Preston, Peter, Jerry, and Garrett. A teacher was sitting with them. Nobody was talking. They were just eating. "Let's not sit with those guys," I said. "I think they're in some kind of trouble."

A bunch of Ginny's friends were sitting together at another table. Katy, Sheena, Linda, and Li were talking and laughing. I don't think any of them had eaten a bite of their lunch yet.

I saw an empty table and a couple of tables that were full of first and second graders. I spotted Donnie Brook's table, too. When I say it's Donnie Brook's table I mean it *is* Donnie Brook's table. Only he and his friends sit there. When he saw me looking he glared and growled at me.

"Well," I said, "how about we *don't* sit at Donnie's table. Let's go sit by Li and the others."

I started walking toward them, but Ginny said, "Wait!" like I was about ready to step off a cliff or something.

"What?"

She was looking across the gymacafeterium, all the way to the back corner. I pretended I didn't see where she was looking. But I knew. She was looking at Eugene Chiver. Eugene was eating alone. Again. Just like he does every single day.

You should know that Eugene Chiver has no friends at school. Once in a while he brings a couple of Big Larry action figures and sets them on the lunch table next to him. He talks to them during lunch. He seems more alone then than when he sits at a totally empty table.

He has more nicknames than any kid you know. Kids call him Space Ranger because he brings his lunch every day in a rusty old lunch box. It has a picture of some TV show from the olden days called *Space Ranger.*

I don't think he got it because he likes the show. I think he got it because it was all they had at the thrift store. Last year when my mom took me and Molly there to shop for Christmas pageant costumes I saw Eugene and his dad looking at it, trying to decide if they should get it.

Sometimes kids call him Liver because it rhymes with his last name, Chiver. Other times we call him Chiver Worst because for lunch every day Eugene has liverwurst sandwiches. You should be happy if you don't know what liverwurst is because it is mashed up liver with all kinds of spices mixed in. And it stinks real bad.

I'm not trying to be mean, but the truth is, Eugene Chiver smells like his liverwurst sandwiches. He even smells like liverwurst before lunch. Whatever shirt he's wearing on Monday will be the shirt he wears each day that week. His hair is never washed or combed. I'm sorry. He's just icky. Which is why Ginny wanted to sit by him during that school lunch taco day.

"He's it," she said. "He's the reason Travel Fish took us to see Jesus eating with sinners and tax collectors."

I had a snappy answer for that. "He's not a tax collector. And maybe eating liverwurst every single day for lunch should be a sin, but I don't think it is."

"Stop it, Johnny! Don't you get it? Eugene is an outcast. Everyone picks on him."

"You don't pick on him," I pointed out to her.

Ginny said, "No. But I don't pay attention to him either. Remember what Bart said?"

"Ummm . . . ," I thought out loud. I thought out loud some more, but I couldn't remember what Bart said.

"Bart said Jesus 'gives the love and forgiveness of God to us and to outcasts. Because he gives those things to me, I will do the same for others, especially for the ones who have been left out by the Pharisees.' Eugene is an outcast, Johnny. It's not good enough to not tease him. We can't forget him, either."

"But there's room at Li's table," I whined.

"There's more room by Eugene," she said.

I knew she was going to sit by him. And I knew I was going to go with her. But I had to try one more time. "If we sit by him everyone will make fun of us, too. They'll have a thousand mean nicknames for each of us. I'll be Johnny Worst and you'll be Ginny Liver Lover!"

Ginny didn't even answer that one. She just started walking toward Eugene Chiver and his empty table. I hung my head and followed her. I knew she was right. Jesus came for people like Eugene just as much as he came for me. But I just knew we were going to get teased by everyone. And I knew that when they were done teasing us, they would tease us some more.

We got to Eugene's table and stood across from him. Ginny—the brave one out of the two of us—spoke first. "May we sit here, Eugene?"

First he just stared at us. Then, very carefully, he said, "Why?" Eugene put his liverwurst sandwich in his rusty "Space Ranger" lunch box and pulled it in close to himself. I noticed a spit wad in his hair that someone had shot at him earlier that day.

"Because . . . ," Ginny had to think hard. "Because these chairs are empty."

Eugene stared at us. His eyes darted back and forth

from Ginny to me, back to Ginny, and back to me again. I think he was waiting for us to call him a name and run away to some other table. When we didn't razz him or run away, he finally said, "Yes." But he said it like a question, like he really didn't trust us. Ginny sat down right next to him. I sat down on the other side of her so that she was between me and Eugene.

By the way, the gymacafeterium—which usually sounds like everybody in the world yelling all at once—was now silent. Even the teachers' table was quiet. Everyone was watching us. Even the lunch ladies in their hairnets couldn't take their eyes off us.

Ginny opened her milk and took a drink. I took a bite of my taco. Eugene nibbled on a corner of his sandwich. People slowly started talking again . . . and laughing. Laughing at us. The top of my head and my cheeks got real hot and kind of tingly.

In a quiet and suspicious voice Eugene asked, "What're you guys doin'?"

"We're eating lunch, Eugene," Ginny said in a singy songy voice.

"Yeah, we're just eating lunch, Eugene," I added.

We all took a few more bites.

"Are you gonna pick on me?" he asked.

When Eugene asked that, my eyes got hot and stingy. "No. We're not gonna pick on you."

"Oh." He looked at the Tato Bites on Ginny's tray and asked her, "Are you gonna eat those?"

"You can have them if you'd like," she answered. Eugene started to pop Tato Bites in his mouth one by one. (Those were supposed to be my Tato Bites!)

The three of us ate the rest of our lunches without saying a word.

It wasn't the end of the world. Our friends still play with us. One day my friend Petey even sat with Eugene and Ginny and me. Other kids did come up with new nicknames. Some people call us the Liverwurst Triplets: Eugene, Euginny, and Eujohnny. Oh well, at least they call Eugene by his real name then.

My Town

Can a dog serve God? Because my dog Stripe visits people at the retirement home and they're sure glad to see him!

Every Thursday Ann and Dean Larson deliver their famous homemade soup to people who live alone at the retirement home.

Our friend Jimmy had his tonsils out and we got to visit him in the hospital.

My mom's friend Linda (she's a nurse) has been very sad lately. Mom hangs out with her and tells her that she belongs to Jesus

This is a place that helps you forgive people (like Donnie Brook) who have been nasty to you.

Some folks from our church visit people in jail. That sounds a little scary, but Pastor Stayput says there are lots of places in the Bible that talk about caring for prisoners.

Here are some ways people serve God in my town.

Where can I serve God?

In my town

Picking up litter is one way to serve.

Do your chores around the house, and try to do them without griping.

Last week Ginny helped a little kid who was lost and couldn't find her mother.

When my sister Molly and I grow enough that we need new clothes, we give old clothes to others who need them.

Stick up for a kid who everyone else ignores or picks on. (My best friend Ginny Stayput is really good at this. I'm getting better.)